The Esse

◆◆

Thomas Hardy
BORN 1840
DIED 1928

The Essential
HARDY

Selected and with an
Introduction by

JOSEPH BRODSKY

The Ecco Press

Thanks to Ann Kjellberg for
her help in compiling the manuscript.

Introduction and selection copyright © 1995 by Joseph Brodsky

Library of Congress Cataloging-in-Publication Data

Hardy, Thomas, 1840–1928.
The essential Hardy / edited with an introduction by Joseph Brodsky.
p.   cm. — (The Essential poets series ; v. 21)
ISBN 0-88001-405-9
I. Brodsky, Joseph, 1940–   . II. Title.   III. Series: Essential poets series
(Hopewell, N.J.) ; 21.
PR4742.B76   1995
821'.8—dc20   94-43654

Contents

The Essential Hardy

Introduction

❖❖

I

A decade or so ago, a prominent English critic, reviewing in an American magazine a collection of poems by the Irish poet Seamus Heaney, remarked that that poet's popularity in Britain, in its academic circles particularly, is indicative of the English public's stolid reading tastes, and that for all the prolonged physical presence of Messieurs Eliot and Pound on British soil, modernism never took root in England. The latter part of his remark (certainly not the former, since in that country—not to mention that milieu—where everyone wishes the other worse off, malice amounts to an insurance policy) got me interested, for it sounded both wistful and convincing.

Shortly afterward, I had the opportunity to meet that critic in person, and although one shouldn't talk shop at the dinner table, I asked him why he thinks modernism faired so poorly in his country. He replied that the generation of poets which could have wrought the decisive change was wiped out in the Great War. I found this answer a bit too mechanistic, considering the nature of the medium, too Marxist, if you will—subordinating literature too much to history. But then the man was a critic, and that's what critics do.

I thought that there must have been another explanation—if not for the fate of modernism on that side of the Atlantic, then for the apparent viability of formal verse there at the present time. Surely there are plenty of reasons for that obvious enough to discard the issue altogether. The sheer pleasure of writing or reading a memorable line would be one; the purely linguistic logic of, and need for, meter and rhyme is another. But nowadays one's mind is conditioned to operate circuitously, and at the time, I thought only that a good rhyme is what in the end saves poetry from becoming a demographic phenomenon. At the time, my thoughts went to Thomas Hardy.

Perhaps I wasn't thinking so circuitously, after all, or at least not yet. Perhaps the expression "Great War" triggered something in my memory, and I remembered Thomas Hardy's "After two thousand years of Mass / We got as far as poison gas." In that case, my thinking was still straight. Or was it perhaps the term "modernism" that triggered those thoughts. In that case... A citizen of a democracy shouldn't be alarmed, of course, to find himself belonging to a minority; though he might get irritable. If a century can be compared to a political system, a significant portion of this one's cultural climate could well qualify as a tyranny: that of modernism. Or, to put it more accurately, of what sailed under that pennant. And perhaps my thoughts went to Hardy because at about that time—a decade ago—he habitually began to be billed as a "pre-modernist."

As definitions go, "pre-modernist" is a reasonably flattering one, since it implies that the so defined has paved the road to our just and happy—stylistically speaking—times. The drawback, though, is that it pensions an author off squarely into the past, offering all the fringe benefits of scholarly interest, of course, but robbing him in effect of relevance. The past tense is his equivalent of a silver watch.

No orthodoxy, especially not a new one, is capable of honest hindsight, and modernism is no exception. While modernism itself presumably benefits from applying this epithet to Thomas Hardy, he, I am afraid, does not. In either case, this definition misleads, for Hardy's poetic output, I daresay, has not so much foreshadowed as overshot, and by an awfully wide margin at that, the development of modern poetry. Had T. S. Eliot, for instance, at the time he read Laforgue, read Thomas Hardy instead (as, for instance, Robert Frost did), the history of poetry in English in this century, or to say the least its present, might be somewhat more absorbing. For one thing, where Eliot needs a handful of dust to perceive terror, for Hardy, as he shows in "Shelley's Skylark," a pinch is enough.

II

All this no doubt sounds to you a touch too polemical. On top of that, you may wonder whom it is that the man in front of you is arguing with. True, the literature on Thomas Hardy is negligible.★ There are two or three full-length studies; they are essentially doctoral-dissertations-turned-books. There are also two or three biographies of the man, including one he penned himself, though it bears his wife's name on the cover. They are worth reading, especially the last, if you believe—as I expect you do— that the artist's life holds the key for understanding his work. If you believe the opposite, you won't lose much by giving them a miss, since we are here to address his work.

I am arguing, I suppose, against seeing this poet through the prism of those who came in his stead. First, because, in most cases, those who came in his stead were operating in relative or absolute ignorance of Hardy the poet's existence—on this side of the Atlantic particularly. The very dearth of literature about

★A Handful of Essays: Robinson, Anden, Stewart, Leavis, Guinen, Tate.

Hardy the poet is both that ignorance's proof and its present echo. Second, because, on the whole, there is little point in reviewing the larger through the prism of the smaller, however vociferous and numerous; our discipline is no astronomy. Mainly, however, because the presence of Hardy the novelist impairs one's eyesight from the threshold, and no critic I know of can resist the temptation to hitch the prose writer to the poet, with the inevitable diminution of the poems as a consequence—if only because the critic's own medium isn't verse.

So to a critic, the prospect of dealing with Hardy's work should look quite messy. To begin with, if one's life holds the key to one's work, as received wisdom claims, then, in Hardy's case, the question is: Which work? Is this or that mishap reflected in this novel, or in that poem, and why not in both? And if a novel, what then is a poem for? And vice versa? Especially since there are about nine novels and roughly a thousand poems in his corpus. Which of these is, should you wax Freudian, a form of sublimation? And how come one keeps sublimating up to the ripe age of eighty-eight, for Hardy kept writing poems to the very end (his last, tenth collection came out posthumously), when the novels are supposed to have done the psychic job? And should one really draw a line between a novelist and poet, or isn't it better to lump them together, echoing Mother Nature?

I say, let's separate them. At any rate, that's what we are going to do in this room. To make a long story short, a poet shouldn't be viewed through any prism other than that of his poems. Besides, technically speaking, Thomas Hardy was a novelist for twenty-six years only. And since he wrote poetry alongside his novels, one could argue that he was a poet for sixty years in a row. To say the least, for the last thirty years of his life; after *Jude the Obscure*—his last and, in my view, his greatest novel—received unfavorable notices, he quit fiction altogether and concentrated on poetry. That alone—the thirty years of verse writing—should be enough to qualify him for the status of a poet. After all, thirty years in this field is an average length for one's career, not to mention life.

So let's give Mother Nature short shrift. Let's deal with the poet's poems. Or, to put it differently, let's bear in mind that human artifice is as organic as any natural masterpiece, which, if we are to believe our naturalists, is also a product of tremendous selection. You see, there are roughly two ways of being natural in this world. One is to strip down to one's underthings, or beyond, and get exposed, as it were, to the elements. That would be, say, a Lawrentian approach, adopted in the second half of this century by many a scribbling dimwit, in our parts, I regret to inform you, especially. The other approach is best exemplified by the following four-liner, written by the great Russian poet Osip Mandelstam:

> *Rome is but nature's twin, which has reflected Rome.*
> *We see its civic might, the signs of its decorum*
> *In the transparent air, the firmament's blue dome,*
> *The colonnades of groves and in the meadow's forum.*

Mandelstam is a Russian, as I said. Yet this quatrain comes in handy because oddly enough it has more to do with Thomas Hardy than anything by D. H. Lawrence, a Brit.

Anyway, at the moment I'd like to go with you through several poems by Mr. Hardy, which by now I hope you have memorized. We'll go through them line by line, so that, apart from whetting your appetite for this poet, you'll be able to see the process of selection that occurs in the course of composition, and that echoes and—if you don't mind my saying so—outshines the similar processes described in the *Origin of Species,* if only because the latter's net result is us, not Mr. Hardy's poems. So let me succumb to the perfectly Darwinian, logical as well as chronological temptation to address the poems belonging to the aforementioned thirty-year period, i.e., to the poems written by Thomas Hardy in the second part of his career, which also means in our century: this way, we leave the novelist behind.

III

Thomas Hardy was born in 1840 and died in 1928. His father was a stonemason and could not afford to support him in a scholarly career, apprenticing him instead to a local church architect. He studied Greek and Latin classics on his own, however, and wrote in his off-hours until the success of *Far from the Madding Crowd* allowed him to quit the job at the age of thirty-four. Thus, his literary career, which started in 1871, allows itself to be fairly neatly divided into two almost even parts: into the Victorian and modern periods, since Queen Victoria conveniently dies in 1901. Bearing in mind that both terms are but catchwords, we'll nevertheless use them for reasons of economy, in order to save ourselves some breath. We shouldn't scrutinize the obvious; as regards our poet, the word "Victorian" catches in particular Robert Browning, Matthew Arnold, George Meredith, both Rossettis, Algernon Swinburne, and, conceivably, Gerard Manley Hopkins and A. E. Housman. To these you might add Charles Darwin himself, Carlyle, Disraeli, John Stuart Mill, Ruskin, Samuel Butler, Walter Pater. But let's stop here: that should give you the general idea of the mental and stylistic parameters—or pressures—pertinent at the time for our poet. Let's leave Cardinal Newman out of it, because our man was a biological determinist and agnostic; let's also leave out the Brontë sisters, Dickens, Thackeray, Trollope, Robert Louis Stevenson, and other fiction writers, because they mattered to Mr. Hardy when he was one of them but not, for instance, when he set out to write "The Darkling Thrush," which is our first poem.

I leant upon a coppice gate
　　When Frost was spectre-gray,
And Winter's dregs made desolate
　　The weakening eye of day.
The tangled bine-stems scored the sky
　　Like strings of broken lyres,
And all mankind that haunted nigh
　　Had sought their household fires.

The land's sharp features seemed to be
　　The Century's corpse outleant,
His crypt the cloudy canopy,
　　The wind his death-lament.
The ancient pulse of germ and birth
　　Was shrunken hard and dry,
And every spirit upon earth
　　Seemed fervourless as I.

At once a voice arose among
　　The bleak twigs overhead
In a full-hearted evensong
　　Of joy illimited;
An aged thrush, frail, gaunt, and small,
　　In blast-beruffled plume,
Had chosen thus to fling his soul
　　Upon the growing gloom.

So little cause for carolings
    Of such ecstatic sound
Was written on terrestrial things
    Afar or nigh around,
That I could think there trembled through
    His happy good-night air
Some blessed Hope, whereof he knew
    And I was unaware.

Now, although this thirty-two line job is Thomas Hardy's most anthologized poem, it is not exactly the most typical of him, being extremely fluent. And that's why perhaps it's so frequently anthologized; although, save for one line in it, it could have been written by practically anyone of talent and, well, insight. These properties were not so rare in English poetry, at the turn of the century especially. It is a very fluent, very lucid poem; its texture is smooth and its structure is conservative enough to hark back to the ballad; its argument is clear and well sustained. In other words, there is very little here of vintage Hardy, and now is as good a time as any lying ahead to tell you what vintage Hardy is like.

Vintage Hardy is a poet who, according to his own admission, "abhorred the smooth line." That would sound perverse were it not for six centuries of verse writing predating his, and were it not for somebody like Tennyson breathing down his neck. Come to think of it, his attitude wasn't very dissimilar from that of Hopkins, and the ways they went about it were, I daresay, not that different, either. At any rate, Thomas Hardy is indeed by and large the poet of a very crammed, overstressed line, filled with clashing consonants, yawning vowels; of an extremely crabby syntax and awkward, cumbersome phrasing aggravated by his seemingly indiscriminate vocabulary; of eye/

ear/mind-boggling stanzaic designs unprecedented in their never-repeating patterns.

So why push him on us, you may ask. Because all this was deliberate and, in the light of what transpired in the English poetry of the rest of this century, quite prophetic. To begin with, the intended awkwardness of Hardy's lines wasn't just the natural striving of a new poet toward a distinct diction, although it played that role, too. Nor should this roughness of surface be seen only as a rebellion against the tonal loftiness and polish of the post-Romantics. In fact, these properties of the post-Romantics are quite admirable, and the whole thesis that Hardy, or anyone else for that matter, "rebelled against" them should be taken with a grain of salt, if taken at all. I think there is another, more down-to-earth as well as more metaphysical explanation for Hardy's stylistic idiom, which in itself was both down-to-earth and metaphysical.

Well, metaphysics is always down-to-earth, isn't it? The more down-to-earth, the more metaphysical, for the things of this world and their interplay are the farthest limit of observation, the language in which matter manifests itself. And the syntax of this language is very crabby indeed. Be that as it may, what Hardy was really after in his verse was, I think, the effect of verisimilitude, the sense of veracity, or, if you will, of authenticity in his speech. The more awkward, he presumably thought, the more true it sounds. Or, at least, the less artful, the more true. Here, perhaps, we should recall that he was also a novelist —though I hope we bring this up for the last time. And novelists think of such things, don't they? Or let's put it a bit more dramatically: he was the kind of man who would think of such things and that's what made him a novelist. However, the man who became a novelist was, before and after that, a poet.

And here we come close to something crucial for our understanding of Hardy the poet; to our sense of what kind of man he was or, more exactly, what kind of mind he had. For the moment, I am afraid, you have to take my assessment for granted; but I hope that within the next half hour it will be borne out by his lines. So here we go: Thomas Hardy, I think, was an extraordinarily perceptive and cunning man. I say "cunning" here without negative connotations, but perhaps I'd better say "plotting." For he indeed plots his poems: not like novels, but precisely as poems. In other words, he knows from the threshold what a poem is, what it should be *like;* he has a certain idea of what his lines should add up to. Nearly every one of his works can be fairly neatly dissected into exposition/argument/denouement, not so much because they were actually structured that way as because structuring was instinctive to Hardy. It comes, as it were, from within the man and reflects not so much his familiarity with the contemporary poetic scene as—as is often the case with autodidacts—his reading of the Greek and Roman classics.

The strength of this structuring instinct in him also explains why Hardy never progressed as a stylist, why his manner never changed. Save for the subject matter, his early poems might sit very comfortably in his late collections, and vice versa. His strongest faculty, moreover, was not the ear but the eye, and the poems existed for him, I believe, more as printed than as spoken matter; had he read his poems aloud, he'd have stumbled himself, but I doubt he would have felt embarrassed and attempted improvements. To put it differently, the real seat of poetry for him was in his mind. No matter how public some of his poems seem, they amount to mental pictures of public address rather than ask for actual delivery. Even the most lyrical of his pieces are essentially mental gestures toward what we know as lyricism in poetry, and they stick to paper more readily than they move your lips. It's hard to imagine Mr. Hardy mouthing his lines into a microphone; but then, I believe, microphones hadn't yet been invented.

So why push him on you, you may persist. Because precisely this voicelessness, this audial neutrality, if you will, and this predominance of the rational over emotional immediacy turn Hardy into a prophetic figure in English poetry: that's what its future liked. In an odd way, his poems have the feeling of being detached from themselves, of not so much being poems as maintaining the appearance of being poems. Herein lies a new aesthetics, an aesthetics insisting on art's conventions not for the sake of emphasis or self-assertion but the other way around: as a sort of camouflage, for better merging with the background against which art exists. Such aesthetics expand art's domain and allow it to land a better punch when and where it's least expected. This is where modernism goofed, but let's let bygones be bygones.

You shouldn't conclude, though, because of what I've told you, that Hardy is heady stuff. As a matter of fact, his verse is entirely devoid of arcana. What's unique about him is, of course, his extraordinary appetite for the infinite, and it appears that, rather than hampering it, the constraints of convention only whet it more. But that's what constraints do to a normal, i.e., not that self-centered, intelligence; and the infinite is poetry's standard turf. Other than that, Hardy the poet is a reasonably easy proposition; you don't need any special philosophical warm-up to appreciate him. You may even call him a realist, because his verse captures an enormous amount of the physical and psychological reality of the time he lived in, of what is loosely called Victorian England.

And yet you wouldn't call him Victorian. Far more than his actual chronology, the aforesaid appetite for the infinite makes him escape this and, for that matter, any definition save that of a poet. Of a man who's got to tell you something about your life no matter where and when he lived his. Except that with Hardy, when you say "poet" you see not a dashing raconteur or a tubercular youth feverishly scribbling in the haze and heat of inspiration but a clear-eyed, increasingly crusty man, bald and of medium height, with a mustache and an aquiline profile, carefully plotting his remorseless, if awkward lines upstairs in his studio, occasionally laughing at the achieved results.

I push him on you in no small part because of that laughter. To me, he casts a very modern figure, and not only because his lines contain a higher percentage of existential truth than his contemporaries', but because of these lines' unmistakable self-awareness. It is as though his poems say to you: Yes, we remember that we are artifacts, so we are not trying to seduce you with our truth; actually, we don't mind sounding a bit quaint. If nevertheless, boys and girls, you find this poet hard going, if his diction appears to you antiquated, keep in mind that the problem may be with you rather than with the author. There is no such thing as antiquated diction, there are only reduced vocabularies. That's why, for example, there is no Shakespeare nowadays on Broadway; apparently the modern audience has more trouble with the bard's diction than the folks at the Globe had. That's progress for you, then; and there is nothing sillier than retrospection from the point of view of progress. And now, off to "The Darkling Thrush."

IV

"The Darkling Thrush" is, of course, a turn-of-the-century poem. But suppose we didn't look at the date beneath it; suppose we opened a book and read it cold. People normally don't look at the dates beneath poems; on top of that, Hardy wasn't all that systematic about dating his work. Imagine, then, reading it cold and catching the date only in the end. What would you say it's all about?

You'd say it's a nature poem, a description of a landscape. On a cold gray winter day a man strolls through a landscape, you would say; he stops and takes in the view. It's a picture of desolation enlivened by the sudden chirping of a bird, and that lifts his spirits. That's what you would say, and you would be right; moreover, that's what the author wants you to think; why, he practically insists on the ordinariness of the scene.

Why? Because he wants you eventually to learn that a new century, a new era—anything new—starts on a gray day, when your spirits are low and there is nothing eye-arresting in sight. That in the beginning there is a gray day, and not exactly a Word. (In about six years you'll be able to check whether or not he was right.) For a turn-of-the-century poem, "The Darkling Thrush" is remarkably unemphatic and devoid of millenarian hoopla. It is so much so that it almost argues against its own chronology; it makes you wonder whether the date wasn't put below the poem afterward, with the benefit of hindsight. And knowing him, one can easily imagine this, for the benefit of hindsight was Hardy's strong suit.

Be that as it may, let's go on with this nature poem, let's fall into his trap. It all starts with "coppice" in the first line. The precision in the naming of this particular type of growth calls the reader's—especially a modern one's—attention to itself, implying the centrality of natural phenomena to the speaker's mind as well as his affinity with it. It also creates an odd sense of security at the poem's opening, since a man familiar with the names of thickets, hedges, and plants can't, almost by definition, be fierce or, in any case, dangerous. That is, the voice we are hearing in the first line is that of nature's ally, and this nature, his diction implies, is by and large human-friendly. Besides, he is leaning on that coppice gate, and a leaning posture seldom bodes even mental aggression; if anything, it's rather receptive. Not to mention that the "coppice gate" itself suggests a nature reasonably civilized, accustomed, almost on its own accord, to human traffic.

The "spectre-gray" in the second line might perhaps put us on alert, were it not for the run-of-the-mill alternation of tetrameters with trimeters, with their balladlike, folk-tune echo, which plays down the ghostliness of "spectre" to the point that we hear "spectrum" more than "spectre," and our mind wanders to the realm of colors rather than homeless souls. What we get out of this line is the sense of controlled melancholy, all the more so since it establishes the poem's meter. "Gray," sitting here in the rhyming position, releases, as it were, the two *e*'s of "spectre" into a sort of exhaling sigh. What we hear is a wistful *eih,* which, together with the hyphen here, turns "shade" into a tint.

The next two lines, "And Winter's dregs made desolate / The weakening eye of day," in the same breath clinch the quatrain pattern which is going to be sustained throughout this thirty-two-line poem and tell you, I am afraid, something about this poet's general view of humanity, or at least of its habitats. The distance between that weakening eye of day, which is presumably the sun, and those winter dregs makes the latter hug, as it were, the ground and take on "Winter"'s implied white or, as the case may be, gray color. I have the distinct feeling that our poet beholds here village dwellings, that we have here a view of a valley, harking back to the old trope of the human spectacle distressing the planets. The dregs, of course, are nothing but residue, what's left when the good stuff has been drunk out of the cup. On top of that, the "Winter's dregs" conjunction gives you a sense of a poet resolutely exiting Georgian diction and standing with both feet in the twentieth century.

Well, at least one foot, as befits a poem written at the turn of the century. One of the additional pleasures of reading Hardy is observing the constant two-step of the contemporary (which is to say, traditional) and his own (which is to say, modern) diction. Rubbing these things against one another in a poem is how the future invades the present and, for that matter, the past to which the language has grown accustomed. In Hardy, this friction of stylistic tenses is palpable to the point of making you feel that he makes no meal of any, particularly his own, modern, stylistic mode. A really novel breakthrough line can easily be followed by a succession of jobs so antiquated you may forget their antecedent altogether. Take, for instance, the second quatrain of the first stanza in "The Darkling Thrush":

> *The tangled bine-stems scored the sky*
>> *Like strings of broken lyres,*
> *And all mankind that haunted nigh*
>> *Had sought their household fires.*

The relatively advanced imagery of the first line (similar, in fact, to the opening passage in Frost's "Woodpile") deteriorates into a fin-de-siècle simile that even at the time of this poem's composition would have given off a stale air of pastiche. Why doesn't our poet strive here for fresher diction, why is he settling for obviously Victorian—even Wordsworthian—tropes, why doesn't he try to get ahead of his time—something he is clearly capable of?

First, because poetry is not a rat race yet. Second, because at the moment, the poem is at the stage of exposition. The exposition of a poem is the most peculiar part, since at this point most poets don't know which way the poem will go. Hence, expositions tend to be long, with English poets especially, and in the nineteenth century in particular. On the whole, across the Atlantic, they have a greater set of references, while over here we've got to look mainly after ourselves. Add to this the pure pleasure of verse writing, of working all sorts of echoes into your texture, and you'll realize that the notion of somebody being "ahead of his time," for all its complimentary ring, is essentially the benefit of hindsight. In the second quatrain of the first stanza, Hardy is squarely behind his time, and he doesn't mind this in the least.

In fact, he loves it. The chief echo here is of the ballad, a term derived from *ballare*, to dance. This is one of the cornerstones of Hardy's poetics. Somebody should calculate the percentage of ballad-based meters in this poet's output; it may easily pass fifty. The explanation for this is not so much young Thomas Hardy's habit of playing the fiddle at country fairs as the English ballad's proclivity for gore and comeuppance, its inherent air of *danse macabre*. The chief attraction of ballad tunes is precisely their dancing—playful, if you insist—denomination, which proclaims from the threshold its artifice. A ballad—and, by extension, a ballad-based meter—announces to the reader: Look, I am not entirely for real; and poetry is too old an art not to use this opportunity for displaying self-awareness. So the prevalence of this sort of tune, in other words, simply coincides—"overlaps" is a better verb—in Hardy with the agnostic's worldview, justifying along the way an old turn of phrase ("haunted nigh") or a trite rhyme ("lyres" / "fires"), except that "lyres" should alert us to the self-referential aspect of the poem.

And as that aspect goes, the next stanza is full of it. It is a fusion of exposition and statement of theme. The end of a century is presented here as the death of a man lying, as it were, in state. To appreciate this treatment better, we have to bear in mind Thomas Hardy's other trade: that of ecclesiastical architect. In that respect, he undertakes here something quite remarkable when he puts the corpse of time into the church of the elements.

What makes this undertaking congenial to him in the first place is the fact that the century's sixty years are his own. In a sense, he owns both the edifice and a large portion of its contents. This dual affinity stems not only from the given landscape at the given season but also from his practiced self-deprecation, all the more convincing in a sixty-year-old.

> *The ancient pulse of germ and birth*
> > *Was shrunken hard and dry,*
> *And every spirit upon earth*
> > *Seemed fervourless as I.*

That he had some twenty-eight years to go (in the course of which, at the age of seventy-four, he remarried) is of no consequence, as he couldn't be aware of such a prospect. An inquisitive eye may even zero in on "shrunken" and perceive a euphemistic job in that "pulse of germ and birth." That would be both reductive and irrelevant, however, since the mental gesture of this quatrain is far grander and more resolute than any personal lament. It ends with "I," and the gaping cæsura after "fervourless" gives this "as I" terrific singularity.

Now the exposition is over, and had the poem stopped here, we'd still have a good piece, the kind of sketch from nature with which the body of many a poet's work swells. For many poems, specifically those that have nature as their subject, are essentially extended expositions fallen short of their objective; sidetracked, as it were, by the pleasure of the attained texture.

Nothing of the sort ever happens in Hardy. He seems always to know what he is after, and pleasure for him is neither a principle nor a valid consideration in verse. He is not big on sonority and orchestrates his lines rather poorly, until it comes to the punch line of the poem, the main point the poem is trying to

score. That's why his expositions are not particularly melliflu-
ous; if they are—as is the case in "The Darkling Thrush"—it is
more by fluke than by intent. With Hardy, the main adventure of
a poem is always toward its end. By and large, he gives you the
impression that verse for him is but the means of transportation,
justified and perhaps even hallowed only by the poem's destina-
tion. His ear is seldom better than his eye, but both are inferior to
his mind, which subordinates them to its purposes, at times
harshly.

So what we've got by now is a picture of utter desolation, of
a man and a landscape locked in their respective moribundity.
The next stanza offers a key:

> At once a voice arose among
> > The bleak twigs overhead
> In a full-hearted evensong
> > Of joy illimited;

This is a treasure trove of a stanza for anyone interested in
Hardy. Let's take its story line at face value and see what our poet
is up to. He is up to showing you an exit out of the previous
stanza's dead end. Dead ends can be exited only upward or by
backing out. "Arose" and "overhead" tells you the route our
poet chooses. He goes for a full-scale elevation here; in fact, for
an epiphany, for a complete takeoff with clear-cut ecclesiastical
connotations. But what is remarkable about this takeoff is the
self-consciousness accompanying the lyrical release of "In a full-
hearted evensong / Of joy illimited." This self-consciousness is
apparent in the dactylic undercutting you detect in both
"evensong" and "illimited": these words come to you prefaced
by a caesura and as though exhaled; as though these lines that be-
gin as assertions dissipate in his throat into qualifiers.

This reflects not so much the understandable difficulty an agnostic may have with ecclesiastical vocabulary as Hardy's true humility. In other words, the takeoff of belief is checked here by the gravity of the speaker's reservations as to his right to use these means of elevation. "An aged thrush, frail, gaunt, and small, / In blast-beruffled plume" is, of course, Hardy's self-portrait. Famous for his aquiline profile, with a tuft of hair hovering above his bald pate, he had indeed a birdlike appearance—in his old age especially, judging by the available photographs. ("Gaunt" is his pet word, a signature really, if only because it is so un-Georgian.)

At any rate, the bird here, in addition to behaving like a bard, has his visual characteristics also. This is our poet's ticket into its sentiments, which yields one of the greatest lines in English poetry of the twentieth century.

It turns out that an aged thrush of not particularly fetching appearance

> Had chosen thus to fling his soul
> Upon the growing gloom.

Speaking of choices, "fling" can't be beaten here. Given the implied visual similarity between bird and bard, this two-liner bespeaking a posture toward reality of the one does the same for another. And if one had to define the philosophy underlying this posture, one would end up no doubt oscillating madly between epicurianism and stoicism. Blissfully, for us terminology is not the most pressing issue. Far more pressing is the need to absorb this two-liner into our system, say for the dark time of the year.

Had the poem stopped here, we would have an extraordinary piece of moral instruction; they are few and far between in poetry but they still do exist. Besides, the superiority of the animal kingdom (birds in particular) in poetry is taken for granted. In fact, the notion of that superiority is one of poetry's most distinctive trappings. What is quite remarkable about "The Darkling Thrush" is that the poet goes practically against this notion, which he himself has bought and is trying to resell in the process of the poem. What's more, by doing this, he almost goes against his most successful lines ever. What is he hoping for? What is he driven by?

Hard to tell, except that perhaps he does not recognize his own success, and what blinds him to it is his metaphysical appetite. Another explanation for why he goes for the fourth stanza here is that appetite's close relative: the sense of symmetry. Those who write formal verse will always prefer four eight-line stanzas to three, and we shouldn't forget the ecclesiastical architect in Hardy. Quatrains could be likened to euphonic building blocks. As such they tend to generate an order that is most satisfactory when it can be divided by four. The sixteen-line exposition naturally—for our poet's mind, ear, and eye—calls for at minimum the same number of lines for the rest.

To put it less idiosyncratically, the stanzaic pattern employed in a poem determines its length as much as—if not more than—its story line. "So little cause for carolings / Of such ecstatic sound" is no less a denouement than the euphonic imperative created by the preceding twenty-four lines, requiring resolution. A poem's length, in other words, is its breath. The first stanza inhales, the second exhales, the third stanza inhales... Guess what you need a fourth stanza for? To complete the cycle.

Remember that this is a poem about looking into the future. As such, it has to be balanced. Our man, poet though he is, is not a utopian; nor can he permit himself the posture of a prophet, or that of a visionary. The subject itself, by definition, is too pregnant with imprecision; so what's required of the poet here is sobriety, regardless of whether he is pessimistic or optimistic by temperament. Hence the absolutely remarkable linguistic content of the fourth stanza, with its fusion of legalese ("cause... Was written") with modernist detachment ("on terrestrial things") and the quaintly archaic ("Afar or nigh around").

"So little cause for carolings / Of such ecstatic sound / Was written on terrestrial things" betrays not so much the unique bloody-mindedness of our poet as his impartiality to any level of diction he resorts to in a poem. There is something frighteningly democratic in Hardy's whole approach to poetics, and it can be summed up as "so long as it works."

Note the elegiac opening of this stanza, all the more poignant in tone because of the "growing gloom" a line before. The pitch is still climbing up, we are still after an elevation, after an exit from our cul-de-sac. "So little cause"—[caesura]—"for carolings / Of such ecstatic"—caesura—"sound..." "Ecstatic" carries an exclamation, and so, after the caesura, does "sound."

Vocally, this is the highest point in the stanza; even "whereof he knew / And I was unaware" is several notes—notches—lower. And yet even at this highest point, the poet, we realize, holds his voice in check, because "carolings / Of such ecstatic sound" are what "a full-hearted evensong" comes down to; which is to say, the evaluation of the bird's voice has undergone a demotion, with ecclesiastical diction being supplanted, as it were, by lay parlance. And then comes this terrific "Was written on terrestrial things," whose detachment from any particularity bespeaks presumably the vantage point either of the "weakening eye of day" or, to say the least, of the bird itself, and that's why we have the archaic—which is to say, impersonal—"Afar or nigh around."

The unparticularity and impersonality, however, belong to neither, but rather their fusion, the crucible being the poet's mind or, if you will, the language itself. Let's dwell on this extraordinary line—"Was written on terrestrial things"—a bit longer, for it crept into this turn-of-the-century poem out of where no poet had ever been before.

The conjunction "terrestrial things" suggests a detachment whose nature is not exactly human. The point of view attained here through the proximity of two abstract notions is, strictly speaking, inanimate. The only evidence of human manufacture is that it is indeed being "written"; and it gives you a sense that language is capable of arrangements that reduce a human being to, at best, the function of a scribe. That it is language that utilizes a human being, not the other way around. That language flows into the human domain from the realm of nonhuman truths and dependencies, that it is ultimately the voice of inanimate matter, and that poetry just registers now and then its ripple effect. And Hardy gives the nod to his inferior status in this transaction when he identifies the "blessed Hope" whereof the situation—the poem—knew as one of which he was unaware.

I am far from suggesting that this is what Thomas Hardy was after in this line. Rather, it was what this line was after in Thomas Hardy, and he responded. And as though he was somewhat perplexed by what escaped from under his pen, he tried to domesticate it by resorting to familiarly Victorian diction in "Afar or nigh around." Yet the diction of this conjunction was destined to become the diction of twentieth-century poetry, more and more. It is only two or three decades from "terrestrial things" to Auden's "necessary murder" of the "artificial wilderness." For its "terrestrial things" line alone, "The Darkling Thrush" is a turn-of-the-century poem.

And the fact that Hardy responded to the inanimate voice of this conjunction had to do obviously with his being well prepared to heed this sort of thing, not only by his agnosticism (which might be enough), but by practically any poem's vector upward, by its gravitation toward epiphany. In principle, a poem goes down the page as much as it goes up in spirit, and "The Darkling Thrush" adheres to this principle closely. On this course, irrationality is not an obstacle, and the ballad's tetrameters and trimeters bespeak a considerable familiarity with irrationality:

> That I could think there trembled through
> > His happy good-night air
> Some blessed Hope, whereof he knew
> > And I was unaware.

What brings our author to this "blessed Hope" is above all the centrifugal momentum developed by the amassment of thirty alternating tetrameters and trimeters, requiring either vocal or mental resolution, or both. In this sense, this turn-of-the-century poem is very much about itself, about its composition which—by happy coincidence—gravitates toward its finale the way the century does. A poem, in fact, offers a century its own, not necessarily rational, version of the future, thereby making the century possible. Against all odds, against the absence of "cause."

And the century—which is soon to be over—has gallantly paid this poem back, as we see in this classroom. In any case, as prophecies go, "The Darkling Thrush" has proved to be more sober and accurate than, let's say, "The Second Coming," by Mr. W. B. Yeats. A thrush proved a more reliable source than a falcon; perhaps because this thrush showed up for Mr. Hardy some twenty years earlier. Perhaps because monotony is more in tune with time's own idiom than a shriek.

So if "The Darkling Thrush" is a poem about nature, it is so only by half, since both bard and bird are that nature's effects, and only one of them is, to put it coarsely, hopeful. It is, rather, a poem about two perceptions of the same reality, and as such it is clearly a philosophical lyric. There is no hierarchy here between hope and hopelessness, distributed in the poem with notable evenhandedness—certainly not between their carriers, as our thrush, I am tempted to point out, is not "aged" for nothing. It's been around, and its "blessed Hope" is as valid as the absence thereof. The last line's caesura isolating "unaware" is eloquent enough to muffle out regret and bring to the last word an air of assertion. After all, the "blessed Hope" is that for the future; that's why the last word here is spoken by reason.

V

Twelve years later—but still before the Irish bard's beast set out for Bethlehem—the British passenger liner *Titanic* sank on her maiden voyage in the mid-Atlantic after colliding with an iceberg. Over 1,500 lives were lost. That was presumably the first of many disasters the century ushered in by Thomas Hardy's thrush became famous for.

"The Convergence of the Twain" was written barely two weeks after the catastrophe; it was published shortly afterward, on May 14. The *Titanic* was lost on April 14. In other words, the raging controversy over the cause of the disaster, the court case against the company, the shocking survivors' accounts, etc.—all those things were still ahead at the time of this poem's composition. The poem thus amounts to a visceral response on the part of our poet; what's more, the first time it was printed, it was accompanied by a headnote saying, "Improvised on the Loss of the *Titanic*."

So, what chord did this disaster strike in Mr. Hardy? "The Convergence of the Twain" is habitually billed by the critical profession either as the poet's condemnation of modern man's self-delusion of technological omnipotence or as the song of his vainglory's and excessive luxury's comeuppance. To be sure, the poem is both. The *Titanic* itself was a marvel of both modern shipbuilding and ostentatiousness. However, no less than in the ship, our poet seems to be interested in the iceberg. And it is the iceberg's generic—triangular—shape that informs the poem's stanzaic design. So does "A Shape of Ice"'s animate nature vis-à-vis the poem's content.

At the same time, it should be noted, the triangular shape suggests the ship: by alluding to the standard representation of a sail. Also, given our poet's architectural past, this shape could connote for him an ecclesiastical edifice or a pyramid. (After all, every tragedy presents a riddle.) In verse, the foundation of such a pyramid would be hexameter, whose caesura divides its six feet into even threes: practically the longest meter available and one Mr. Hardy was particularly fond of, perhaps because he taught himself Greek.

Although his fondness for figurative verse (which comes to us from Greek poetry of the Alexandrian period) shouldn't be overstated, his enterprise with stanzaic patterns was great enough to make him sufficiently self-conscious about the visual dimension of his poems to make such a move. In any case, the stanzaic design of "The Convergence of the Twain" is clearly deliberate, as two trimeters and one hexameter (normally conveyed in English precisely by two trimeters—also the convergence of a twain) show, held together by the triple rhyme.

I

In a solitude of the sea
Deep from human vanity,
And the Pride of Life that planned her, stilly couches she.

II

Steel chambers, late the pyres
Of her salamandrine fires,
Cold currents thrid, and turn to rhythmic tidal lyres.

III

Over the mirrors meant
To glass the opulent
The sea-worm crawls—grotesque, slimed, dumb, indifferent.

IV

Jewels in joy designed
To ravish the sensuous mind
Lie lightless, all their sparkles bleared and black and blind.

V

Dim moon-eyed fishes near
Gaze at the gilded gear
And query: "What does this vaingloriousness down here?"

VI

Well: while was fashioning
This creature of cleaving wing,
The Immanent Will that stirs and urges everything

VII

Prepared a sinister mate
For her—so gaily great—
A Shape of Ice, for the time far and dissociate.

VIII

And as the smart ship grew

> In stature, grace, and hue
> In shadowy silent distance grew the Iceberg too.

IX

> Alien they seemed to be:
> No mortal eye could see
> The intimate welding of their later history,

X

> Or sign that they were bent
> By paths coincident
> On being anon twin halves of one august event,

XI

> Till the Spinner of the Years
> Said "Now!" And each one hears,
> And consummation comes, and jars two hemispheres.

This is a bona fide occasional poem in the form of a public address. In fact, it is an oration; it gives you the feeling that it should be spoken from a pulpit. The opening line—"In a solitude of the sea"—is extraordinarily spacious, both vocally and visually, suggesting the width of the sea's horizon—we are in one of its many solitudes—and that degree of elemental autonomy which is capable of perceiving its own solitude.

But if the opening line scans the vast surface, the second line—"Deep from human vanity"—takes you farther away from the human sphere, straight into the heart of this utterly isolated element. In fact, the second line is an invitation for the underwater journey which is what the first half of the poem—a lengthy exposition again!—amounts to. Toward the end of the third line, the reader is well along on a veritable scuba-diving expedition.

Trimeters are a tricky proposition. They may be rewarding euphonically, but they naturally constrain the content. At the outset of the poem they help our poet to establish his tonality; but he is anxious to get on with the business of the poem. For this, he gets the third, quite capacious hexametric line, in which he proceeds indeed in a very businesslike, indeed bloody-minded fashion:

And the Pride of Life that planned her, stilly couches she.

The first half of this line is remarkable for its pile up of stresses, no less than for what it ushers in: the rhetorical, abstract construct which is, on top of that, also capitalized. Now, the Pride of Life is of course linked syntactically to human vanity, but this helps matters little because (a) human vanity is not capitalized, and (b) it is still more coherent and familiar a concept than the Pride of Life. Furthermore, the two *n*'s in "that planned her" give you a sense of a truly jammed, bottle neck–type diction, befitting an editorial more than a poem.

No poet in his right mind would try to cram all this into half a line: it is unutterable. On the other hand, as we've noted, there were no mikes. Actually, "And the Pride of Life that planned her," though menaced by its mechanical scansion, can be delivered out loud, to the effect of somewhat unwarranted emphasis; the effort, however, will be obvious. The question is, why does Thomas Hardy do this? And the answer is, because he is confident that the image of the ship resting at the bottom of the sea and the triple rhyme will bail this stanza out.

"Stilly couches she" is indeed a wonderful counterbalance to the unwieldy pile up of stresses ushering it in. The two *l*'s—a "liquid" consonant—in "stilly" almost convey the gently rocking body of the ship. As for the rhyme, it clinches the femininity of the ship, already emphasized by the verb "couches." For the purposes of the poem, this suggestion is indeed timely.

What does our poet's deportment in this stanza and, above all, in its third line tell us about him? That he is a very calculating fellow (at least he counts his stresses). Also, that his pen is driven less by a sense of harmony than by his central idea, and that his triple rhyme is a euphonic necessity second and a structural device first. As rhymes go, what we've got in this stanza is no great shakes. The best that can be said about it is that it is highly functional and reverberates the wonderful fifteenth-century poem sometimes attributed to [William] Dunbar:

> *In what estate so ever I be*
> Timor mortis conturbat me...
> *"All Christian people, behold and see:*
> *This world is but a vanity*
> *And replete with necessity.*
> Timor mortis conturbat me."

It's quite possible that these lines indeed set "The Convergence of the Twain" in motion, because it is a poem above all about vanity and necessity, as well, of course, as about fear of death. However, what perturbs the seventy-two-year-old Thomas Hardy in his poem is precisely necessity.

> *Steel chambers, late the pyres*
> *Of her salamandrine fires,*
> *Cold currents thrid, and turn to rhythmic tidal lyres.*

We are indeed on an underwater journey here, and although the rhymes are not getting any better (we encounter our old friend "lyres"), this stanza is striking because of its visual content. We are clearly in the engine room, and the entire machinery is seen quiveringly refracted by water. The word that really stars in this stanza is "salamandrine." Apart from its mythological and metallurgical connotations, this four-syllable-long, lizardlike epithet marvelously evokes the quivering motion of the element directly opposite to water: fire. Extinguished, yet sustained, as it were, by refractions.

"Cold" in "Cold currents thrid, and turn to rhythmic tidal lyres" underscores this transformation; but on the whole, the line is extremely interesting because it arguably contains a hidden metaphor of the very process of composing this poem. On the surface—or, rather, underneath it—we have the movement of the waves approaching the shore (or a bay, or a cove), which looks like the horn of a lyre. Breakers, then, are its played strings. The verb "thrid," being the archaic (or dialect) form of "thread," while conveying the weaving of the sound and meaning from line to line, euphonically also evokes the triangularity of the stanzaic design, which is a triplet. In other words, with the progression from "fire" to "cold" we get to an artifice which suggests artistic self-consciousness in general and, given the treatment a great tragedy receives in this poem, Hardy's in particular. For, to put it bluntly, "The Convergence of the Twain" is devoid of the "hot" feelings that might seem appropriate, given the volume of human loss. This is an entirely unsentimental job, and in the second stanza our poet reveals somewhat (most likely unwittingly) the way it's done.

> Over the mirrors meant
> To glass the opulent
> The sea-worm crawls—grotesque, slimed, dumb, indifferent.

This is where, I believe, the poem's reputation for social criticism comes from. It is there, of course, but that's the least of it. The *Titanic* was indeed a floating palace. The ballroom, casino, and cabins themselves were built to redefine luxury on the grandest scale, their decor was lavish. To convey this, the poet uses the verb "to glass," which both doubles the opulence and betrays its one-dimensionality: it is glass-deep. However, in the scene Mr. Hardy paints here, he is concerned less, I think, with debunking the rich than with the discrepancy between the intent and the outcome. The sea-worm crawling over the mirror stands in not for the essence of capitalism but for "the opulent"'s opposite. The opposition is the familiar stuff of religion—"Surely every man walketh in a vain shew: surely they are disquieteth in vain: he heapeth up riches, and knoweth not who shall gather them," says the Psalm—but Hardy's catalogue is notably lacking in appeals for celestial relief.

The succession of negative epithets qualifying that sea-worm tells us quite a lot about Mr. Hardy himself. For in order to know the value of a negative epithet, one should always try applying it to oneself first. Being a poet, not to mention a novelist, Thomas Hardy would have done that more than once. Therefore, the succession of negative epithets here could and should be perceived as reflecting his hierarchy of human wrongs, the gravest being the last on the list. And the last on this list, sitting above all in the rhyming position, is "indifferent." This renders "grotesque, slimed, dumb" as lesser evils. At least from the point of view of this poet, they are; and one can't help thinking that the gravity"indifferent" is burdened with in this context is perhaps self-referential.

> *Jewels in joy designed*
> *To ravish the sensuous mind*
> *Lie lightless, all their sparkles bleared and black and blind.*

Perhaps this is as good a time as any to point to the cinematic, frame-by-frame procedure our poet resorts to here, and the fact that he is doing this in 1912, long before film became a daily—well, nightly—reality. I believe I've said someplace that it was poetry that invented the technique of montage, not Eisenstein. A vertical arrangement of identical stanzas on the page *is* a film. A couple of years ago a salvaging company trying to raise the *Titanic* showed its footage of the ship on TV; it was remarkably close to the matter at hand. Their emphasis was obviously on the contents of the ship's vault, which among other things might have contained a manuscript of Joseph Conrad's most recent novel, which was sent by the author to his American publisher with the ship, since it was to be the speediest mail carrier, among other virtues. The camera circled in the vault area incessantly, attracted by the smell of its riches, but to no avail. Thomas Hardy does a far better job.

"Jewels in joy designed" practically glitters with its *j*'s and *s*'s. So does, with its swishing and hissing *s*'s, the next line. Yet the most fascinating use of alliteration is on display in the third line, where the ravished, sensuous mind goes flat, as all the line's *l*'s crackle and burst in "sparkles," turning the jewels in "*bl*eared and *bl*ack and *bl*ind" into so many released bubbles rising to the line's end. The alliteration is literally undoing itself in front of our eyes.

It is more rewarding to admire the poet's ingenuity here than to read into this line a sermon on the ephemeral and destructive nature of riches. Even if the latter were his concern, the emphasis would be on the paradox itself rather than the social commentary. Had Thomas Hardy been fifty years younger at the time of the composition of "The Convergence of the Twain," he perhaps might have sharpened the social edge of the poem a bit more, though even this is doubtful. As it was, he was seventy-two years old, fairly well off himself; and among the 1,500 souls lost when the *Titanic* went down, two were his personal acquaintances. However, on his underwater journey, he is not looking for them either.

> *Dim moon-eyed fishes near*
> *Gaze at the gilded gear*
> *And query: "What does this vaingloriousness down here?"*

"Gaze at the gilded gear" has obviously crept into the second line of this stanza by pure alliterative inertia (the author presumably had other word combinations to consider working up the last stanza, and this is just one of the spin-offs), which serves to reca-pitulate the ship's ostentatiousness. Fish are seen here as if through a porthole, hence the magnifying-glass effect dilating the fish eyes and making them moonlike. Of much greater con-sequence, however, is the stanza's third line, which concludes the exposition and serves as the springboard for the poem's main business.

"And query: "What does this vaingloriousness down here?" is not only a rhetorical turn setting up the rest of the poem to provide the answer to the question posed by the line. It is first of all the recapturing of the oratorical posture, somewhat diluted by the lengthy exposition. To achieve that, the poet heightens his diction here, by combining the legalese of "query" with the clearly ecclesiastical "vaingloriousness." The latter's five-syllable-long hulk marvelously evokes the cumbersomeness of the ship at the sea's bottom. Apart from this, though, both the legalese and the ecclesiastical clearly point to a stylistic shift and a change of the whole discourse's plane of regard.

> *Well: while was fashioning*
> *This creature of cleaving wing,*
> *The Immanent Will that stirs and urges everything*
> *Prepared a sinister mate*
> *For her—so gaily great—*
> *A Shape of Ice, for the time far and dissociate.*

Now, "Well" here both disarms and signals a regrouping. It's a colloquial conceit, designed both to put the audience a bit off guard—should "vaingloriousness" have put it on alert—and to pump some extra air into the speaker's lungs as he embarks on a lengthy, extremely loaded period. Resembling somewhat the speech mannerisms of our fortieth President, "Well" here indicates that the movie part of the poem is over and now the discourse begins in earnest. It appears that the subject, after all, is not submarine fauna but Mr. Hardy's—as well as poetry's very own, ever since the days of Lucretius—principle of causality.

"Well: while was fashioning / This creature of cleaving wing" informs the public—syntactically, above all—that we are beginning from afar. More important, the subordinate clause preceding the Immanent Will statement exploits to the hilt the ship's gender designation in our language. We've got three words here with increasingly feminine connotations, whose proximity to each other adds up to an impression of deliberate emphasis. "Fashioning" could have been a fairly neutral reference to shipbuilding were it not qualified by "this creature," with its overtones of particular fondness, and were "this creature" itself not side-lit by "cleaving." There is more of "cleavage" in "cleaving" than of "cleaver," which, while describing the movement of the ship's prow through the water, also echoes a type of sail with its whiteness like a blade. In any case, the conjunction of "cleaving wing"—and "wing" itself especially, sitting here in the rhyming position—pitches the line sufficiently high for Mr. Hardy to usher in a notion central to his entire mental operation, that of "The Immanent Will that stirs and urges everything."

Hexameter gives this notion's skeptical grandeur full play. The caesura separates the formula from the qualifier in the most natural way, letting us fully appreciate the almost thundering reverberations of consonants in "Immanent Will," as well as the resolute assertiveness "that stirs and urges everything." The latter is all the more impressive thanks to the reserve in the line's dactyls—which borders, in fact, on hesitation—detectable in "everything." Third in the stanza, this line is burdened with the inertia of resolution, and gives you a feeling the entire poem has been written for the sake of this statement.

Why? Because if one could speak of Mr. Hardy's philosophical outlook (if one can speak about a poet's philosophy at all, since, given the omniscient nature of language alone, such discourse is doomed to be reductive by definition), one would have to admit that the notion of Immanent Will was paramount to it. Now, it all harks back to Schopenhauer, with whom the sooner you get acquainted the better—not so much for Mr. Hardy's sake as for your own. Schopenhauer will save you quite a trip; more exactly, his notion of the Will, which he introduced in his *The World as Will and Idea,* will. Every philosophical system, you see, can easily be charged with being essentially a solipsistic, if not downright anthropomorphic, endeavor. By and large they all are, precisely because they are *systems* and thus imply a varying—usually quite high—degree of rationality of overall design. Schopenhauer escapes this charge with his Will, which is his term for the phenomenal world's inner essence; better yet, for a ubiquitous nonrational force and its blind, striving power operating in the world. Its operations are devoid of ultimate purpose or design and are not many a philosopher's incarnations of rational or moral order. In the end, of course, this notion can also be charged with being a human self-projection. Yet it can defend itself better than others with its horrific, meaningless omniscience, permeating all forms of struggle for existence but voiced (from Schopenhauer's point of view, presumably only echoed) by poetry alone. Small wonder that Thomas Hardy, with his appetite for the infinite and the inanimate, zeroed in on this notion: small wonder that he capitalizes it in this line, for whose sake one may think the entire poem was written.

It wasn't:

> Prepared a sinister mate
> For her—so gaily great—
> A Shape of Ice, for the time far and dissociate.

For if you give four stars to that line, how are you to rank "A Shape of Ice, for the time far and dissociate"? Or, for that matter, "a sinister mate"? As conjunctions go, it is so far ahead of 1912! It's straight out of Auden. Lines like that are invasions of the future into the present, they are whiffs of the Immanent Will themselves. The choice of "mate" is absolutely marvelous, since apart from alluding to "shipmate," it again underscores the ship's femininity, sharpened even further by the next trimeter: "For her—so gaily great—"

What we are getting here, with increasing clarity, is not so much collision as a metaphor for romantic union as the other way around: the union as a metaphor for the collision. The femininity of the ship and the masculinity of the iceberg are clearly es-

tablished. Except that it is not exactly the iceberg. The real mark
of our poet's genius is in his offering a circumlocution: "A Shape
of Ice." Its menacing power is directly proportionate to the
reader's ability to fashion that shape according to his own imag-
ination's negative potential. In other words, this circumlocution
—actually, its letter *a* alone—insinuates the reader into the poem
as an active participant.

Practically the same job is performed by "for the time far
and dissociate." Now, "far" as an epithet attached to time is
commonplace; any poet could do it. But it takes Hardy to use in
verse the utterly unpoetic "dissociate." This is the benefit of the
general stylistic nonchalance of his we commented on earlier.
There are no good, bad, neutral words for this poet: they are ei-
ther functional or not. This could be put down, of course, to his
experience with prose, were it not for his frequently stated ab-
horrence of the smooth, "jewelled line."

And "dissociate" is about as unglittering as it is functional.
It bespeaks not only the Immanent Will's farsightedness but
time's own disjointed nature: not in the Shakespearean but in the
purely metaphysical—which is to say, highly perceptible, tactile,
mundane—sense. The latter is what makes any member of the
audience identify with the disaster's participants, placing him or
her within time's atomizing domain. What ultimately saves "dis-
sociate," of course, is its being rhymed, with the attendant aspect
of resolution moreover, in the third, hexametric line.

Actually, in the last two stanzas, the rhymes get better and
better: engaging and unpredictable. To appreciate "dissociate"
fully, perhaps, one should try reading the stanza's rhymes verti-
cally, column-wise. One would end up with "mate—great—
dissociate." This is enough to give one a shudder, and this is far
from being gratuitous, since the succession clearly emerged in
the poet's mind before the stanza was finished. In fact, this was

precisely what allowed him to finish the stanza, and to do it the way he did.

> *And as the smart ship grew*
> *In stature, grace, and hue*
> *In shadowy silent distance grew the Iceberg too.*

And so it emerges that we are dealing with the betrothed. With the feminine smart ship engaged early on to a Shape of Ice. A construction to nature. Almost a brunette to a blonde. Something was growing in Plymouth docks toward that which was growing "In shadowy silent distance" somewhere in the North Atlantic. The hushed, conspiratorial "shadowy silent distance" underscores the secretive, intimate character of this information, and the stresses falling almost mechanically on each word in this stanza sort of echo time's measured pace—the pace of this maid's and her mate's advancement. For it is that pace that makes the encounter inevitable, not the pair's individual features.

What also makes their approach inexorable is the excess of rhyme in this stanza. "Grew" creeps into the third line, making this triplet contain four rhymes. That could be regarded, of course, as a cheap effect, were it not for the rhyme's sound. "Grew—hue—too" has, as a euphonic referent, the word "you," and the second "grew" triggers the reader's realization of his/her involvement in the story, and not as its addressee only.

> *Alien they seemed to be:*
> *No mortal eye could see*
> *The intimate welding of their later history.*

In the euphonic context of the last four stanzas, "Alien" comes as an exclamation, its wide-open vowels like the last cry of the doomed before submitting to the unavoidable. It's like "not guilty" on the scaffold or "I don't love him" before the altar: pale face turned to the public. And the altar it is, for "welding" as well as "history" in the third line sound like homonyms for "wedding" and "destiny." So "No mortal eye could see" is not so much the poet's bragging about being privy to the workings of causality as the voice of a Father Lorenzo.

> *Or sign that they were bent*
> *By paths coincident*
> *On being anon twin halves of one august event.*

Again, no poet in his right mind, unless his is Gerard Manley Hopkins's, would stud a line with stresses in such a hammering manner. And not even Hopkins would dare to use in verse "anon" like this. Is this our old friend Mr. Hardy's abhorrence of the smooth line, reaching here a degree of perversity? Or a further attempt to obscure, with this Middle English equivalent of "at once," a "mortal eye"'s ability to see what he, the poet, sees? An elongation of the perspective? Going for those coincident paths of origin—the only concession to the standard view of the disaster? Or just a heightening of the pitch, the way "august" does, in view of the poem's finale, to pave the way for the Immanent Will's saying its piece:

> *Till the Spinner of the Years*
> *Said "Now!" And each one hears,*
> *And consummation comes, and jars two hemispheres.*

"Everything" that the Immanent Will "stirs and urges" presumably includes time. Hence the Immanent Will's new billing: "Spinner of the Years." This is a bit too personified for the no-

| 41 |

tion's abstract good, but we may put this down to the ecclesiastical architect's inertia in Hardy. He comes uncomfortably close here to equating the meaningless with the malevolent, whereas Schopenhauer pushes precisely the blind mechanistic—which is to say, nonhuman—nature of that Will, whose presence is recognized by all forms of existence, both animate and inanimate, through stress, conflict, tension, and, as in the case at hand, through disaster.

This in the final analysis is what lies behind his poetry's quite ubiquitous predilection for the dramatic anecdote. The nonhumanity of the ultimate truth about the phenomenal world fires up his imagination the way female beauty does many a Lothario's. A biological determinist, on the one hand, he eagerly, as it were, embraces Schopenhauer's notion not only because it amounts in his mind to the source of completely unpredictable and otherwise unaccountable occurrences (unifying thus the "far and dissociate") but also, one suspects, to account for his own "indifference."

You could bill him as a rational irrationalist, of course, but that would be a mistake, since the concept of Immanent Will is not irrational. No, quite the contrary. It is highly uncomfortable, not to say menacing, perhaps; but that is a different matter altogether. Discomfort shouldn't be equated with irrationality any more than rationality with comfort. Still, this is the wrong place for nit-picking. One thing is clear: the Immanent Will for our poet has the status of Supreme Entity, bordering on that of Prime Mover. Fittingly, then, it speaks in monosyllables; fittingly, also, it says: "Now."

The most fitting word in this last stanza, however, is, of course, "consummation," since the collision occurred at night. With "consummation" we have the marital union trope seen, as it were, to the end. "Jars," with its allusion to broken earthenware, is more this trope's residue than its enhancement. It is a stunning verb here, making the two hemispheres, which the "maiden" voyage of the *Titanic* was supposed to connect, into two clashing convex receptacles. It looks as if it was precisely the notion "maiden" that struck the chord of our poet's "lyre" first.

VI

The question is why, and the answer arrives in the form of a cycle of poems written by Mr. Hardy a year after "The Convergence of the Twain," the famous *Poems of 1912–13*. As we are about to embark on discussing one of them, let's bear in mind that the feminine ship was lost and that the masculine Shape of Ice survived the encounter. That the remarkable lack of sentimentality, warranted in principle by both the genre and the subject of the poem, could be attributed to our poet's inability to identify here with the loser, if only because of the ship's gender.

Poems of 1912–13 was occasioned by the poet's loss of his wife of thirty-eight years, Emma Lavinia Gifford, who died on November 27, 1912, eight months after the *Titanic* disaster. Twenty-one pieces in all, these poems amount to the Shape of Ice's meltdown.

To make a long story short, the marriage was long and unhappy enough to give "The Convergence of the Twain" its central metaphor. It was also sufficiently solid to make at least one of its participants regard himself as a plaything of the Immanent Will, and, as such playthings go, a cold one. Had Emma Hardy outlived her husband, this poem would stand as a remarkable, albeit oblique, monument to the morose equilibrium of their dissociate lives, to the low temperature of the poet's heart.

The sudden death of Emma Hardy shattered this equilibrium. In a manner of speaking, the Shape of Ice suddenly found

| 43 |

itself on its very own. In another manner of speaking, *Poems of 1912–13* is essentially this Iceberg's lament for the vanished ship. As such, it is a meticulous reconstruction of the casualty; the by-product, naturally, of an excruciating self-examination rather than a metaphysical quest for the tragedy's origins. After all, no casualty can be redeemed by exposing its causality.

That's why this cycle is essentially retrospective. To make a long story still shorter, its heroine is not Emma Hardy, the wife, but precisely Emma Lavinia Gifford, the bride: a maiden. The poems look at her through the dim prism of forty-three years of marriage, through the foggy hard crystal of Emma Hardy herself. If this cycle has a hero, it is the past with its happiness or, to put it a bit more accurately, with its promise of happiness.

As human predicaments go, the story is sufficiently common. As a subject for elegiac poetry, the loss of the beloved is common as well. What makes *Poems of 1912–13* slightly unusual at the outset is not only the age of the poet and his heroine but the sheer number of poems and their formal variety. A characteristic feature with elegies occasioned by someone's demise is their tonal, to say the least, metric uniformity. In the case of this cycle, however, we have a remarkable metric diversity, which points to the possibility that craftsmanship was a no lesser issue for the poet here than the issue itself.

A psychological explanation for this variety might be, of course, that it has to do with our poet's grief searching for an adequate form of expression. Still, the formal intricacy of the twenty-one attempts made in that direction suggests a greater pressure behind this cycle than pure grief or, for that matter, any single sentiment. So let us take a look at perhaps the least stanzaically enterprising among these poems and try to find out what's going on.

Here by the moorway you returned,
And saw the borough lights ahead
That lit your face—all undiscerned
To be in a week the face of the dead,
And you told of the charm of that haloed view
That never again would beam on you.

And on your left you passed the spot
Where eight days later you were to lie,
And be spoken of as one who was not;
Beholding it with a heedless eye
As alien from you, though under its tree
You soon would halt everlastingly.

I drove not with you . . . Yet had I sat
At your side that eve I should not have seen
That the countenance I was glancing at
Had a last-time look in the flickering sheen,
Nor have read the writing upon your face,
"I go hence soon to my resting-place;

"You may miss me then. But I shall not know
How many times you visit me there,
Or what your thoughts are, or if you go
There never at all. And I shall not care.
Should you censure me I shall take no heed,
And even your praises no more shall need."

True: never you'll know. And you will not mind.
But shall I then slight you because of such?
Dear ghost, in the past did you ever find
The thought "What profit," move me much?
Yet abides the fact, indeed, the same,—
You are past love, praise, indifference, blame.

"Your Last Drive" is the second in the cycle and, according to the date underneath, was written less than a month after Emma Hardy's death, i.e., when the shock of her departure was very fresh. Ostensibly an evocation of her returning home in the evening from a routine outing that proved to be her last, the poem for its first two stanzas appears to explore the paradox of the interplay between motion and stasis. The carriage carrying the heroine past the place where she shortly will be buried seems to arrest the poet's imagination as a metaphor either of mobility's myopic vision of immobility or of space's disregard for either. In any case, the mental input in these stanzas is somewhat larger than the sentimental one, though the latter comes first.

More accurately, the poem strays from the emotional into the rational, and rather quickly so. In this sense, it is indeed vintage Hardy, for the trend is seldom the reverse with him. Besides, every poem is a means of transportation by definition, and this one is only more so, since metrically at least it is about a means of transportation. With its iambic tetrameter and the shifting caesura that makes its fifth line slide into an anapest, its stanza wonderfully conveys the tilting movement of a horse-driven carriage, and the closing couplets mimic its arrival. As is inevitable with Hardy, this pattern is sustained throughout the poem.

We first see the features of the cycle's heroine lit—most likely dimly—by "the borough lights ahead." The lighting here is more cinematic than poetic; nor does the word "borough" heighten the diction much—something you would expect when it comes to the heroine's appearance. Instead, a line and a half are expended on stressing—literally, and with a touch of tautological relish—her lack of awareness of the impending transformation into being "the face of the dead." In effect, her features are absent; and the only explanation for our poet's not grabbing this opportunity to depict them is the prospect of the cycle already existing in his head (although no poet is ever sure of his ability to produce the next poem). What's present of her, however, in this stanza is her speech, echoed in "And you told of the charm of that haloed view." One hears in this line her "It's charming," and conceivably, "Such a halo!" as she was by all accounts a churchgoing woman.

The second stanza sticks to the "moorway" topography no less than to the chronology of events. Apparently the heroine's outing occurred one week—perhaps slightly less—before she died, and she was interred on the eighth day at this place apparently to her left as she drove home by the moorway. Such literalness may owe here to the poet's deliberately reining in his emotion, and "spot" suggests a conscious deflation. It is certainly in keeping with the notion of a carriage trundling along, supported, as it were, by leaf-springs of tetrameters. Yet knowing Hardy's appetite for detail, for the mundane, one may as well assume that no special effort was applied here and no special significance was sought. He simply registers the pedestrian manner in which an absurdly drastic change has taken place.

Hence the next line, which is the highest point in this stanza. In "And be spoken of as one who was not," one detects the sense not so much of loss or unbearable absence as that of all-consuming negation. "One who was not" is too resolute for comfort or, for that matter, for discomfort, and negation of an individual is what death is all about. Therefore, "Beholding it with a heedless eye / As alien from you" is not a scolding but rather an admission of the appropriate response. With ". . . though under its tree / You soon would halt everlastingly" the carriage and the exposition part of the poem indeed come to a halt.

Essentially, the central theme of these two stanzas is their heroine's lack of any inkling or premonition of her approaching end. This could be perceived as a remarkable expectation indeed, were it not for her age. Besides, although throughout the cycle the poet insists on the suddenness of Emma Hardy's demise, it's obvious from other sources that she was afflicted with all sorts of ailments, including a mental disorder. But presumably there was something about her that made him convinced of her durability; perhaps that had to do with his notion of himself as the Immanent Will's plaything.

And although many would regard the third stanza's opening as heralding the theme of guilt and remorse that the same many would detect in the whole cycle, "I drove not with you" is just a restatement of that premonition's requirement: worse comes to worse, of his probable failure at obtaining it. The next line and a half postulate quite resolutely that probability, ruling out grounds for the speaker's self-reproach on that account. Yet for the first time, true lyricism creeps into the poem: first through the ellipsis, secondly through "Yet had I sat / At your side that eve" (which is, of course, a reference to his not being at her side at the moment of death). It takes over in full force with "That the countenance I was glancing at," where all the consonants of "countenance" vibrate, giving you a passenger's silhouette swaying from side to side because of the carriage's movement, seen against the light. The treatment again is quite cinematic, the film being black-and-white. One could throw "*flick*ering" into the bargain, were it not 1912.

And were it not for the starkness of "Had a last-time look" (still, perceptions often run ahead of technology, and as we said earlier, montage wasn't invented by Eisenstein). This starkness both enhances and shatters the almost loving tentativeness of "the countenance I was glancing at," betraying the poet's eagerness to escape a reverie for the truth, as though the latter is more rewarding.

A reverie he certainly escapes, but he pays for that with the monstrous next line: with recalling the heroine's actual features in "Nor have read the writing upon your face." The reference here, obviously, is to the writing upon the wall, whose inescapable equation with the heroine's appearance tells us enough about the state of the union prior to her death. What informs this equation is his sense of her impenetrability, and that's what the poem was all about thus far, since this impenetrability applies to the past about as much as it does to the future, and it's a quality she happens to share with the future generally. Thus his reading of Emma's equivalent of *"Mene, Mene, Tekel, Upharsin"* here is no fantasy.

> *"I go hence soon to my resting-place;*
>
> *"You may miss me then. But I shall not know*
> *How many times you visit me there,*
> *Or what your thoughts are, or if you go*
> *There never at all. And I shall not care.*
> *Should you censure me I shall take no heed,*
> *And even your praises no more shall need."*

Here is our heroine, verbatim. Because of the deftly blended tenses, this is a voice from beyond the grave as much as from the past. And it is relentless. With every next sentence, she takes away what she has given a sentence before. And what she gives and takes is obviously his humanity. This way she reveals herself to be indeed a good match for her poet. There is a strong echo of marital argument in these lines, the intensity of which overcomes completely the listlessness of the verse. It gets much louder here and drowns the sound of the carriage wheels on the cobblestones. To say the least, dead, Emma Hardy is capable of invading her poet's future to the point of making him defend himself.

What we have in this stanza is essentially an apparition. And although the cycle's epigraph—"Traces of an old flame"—is taken from Virgil, this particular passage bears a very close resemblance, both in pitch and substance—to the famous elegy by Sextus Propertius, from his "Cynthia Monobiblos." The last two lines in this stanza, in any case, sound like a good translation of Cynthia's final plea: "And as for your poems in my honor, burn them, burn them!"

The only escape from such negation is into the future, and that's the route our poet takes: "True: never you'll know." That future, however, should be fairly distant, since its foreseeable part, the poet's present, is already occupied. Hence, "And you will not mind" and "But shall I then slight you because of such?" Still, with that escape comes—in this last stanza's first line especially—a piercing recognition of the ultimate parting, of the growing distance. Characteristically, Hardy handles this line with terrific reserve, allowing only a sigh to escape in the caesura and a slight elevation of pitch in "mind." Yet the suppressed lyricism bursts into the open and claims its own in "Dear ghost."

He indeed addresses an apparition, but one that's free of any ecclesiastical dimension. This is not a particularly mellifluous form of address, which alone convinces one of its literalness. He is not searching here for a tactful alternative. (What could there be instead? The meter, allotting him here only two syllables, rules out "Dear Emma"; what then, "Dear friend"?) A ghost she is, and not because she is dead, but because though less than a physical reality she is far more than just a memory: she is an entity he can address, a presence—or absence—he is familiar with. It's not the inertia of marriage but of time itself—thirty-eight years of it—that solidifies into a substance that may be, he feels, only hardened by his future, which is but another increment of time.

Hence, "Dear ghost." Thus designated, she can almost be touched. Or else "ghost" is the ultimate in detachment. And for somebody who ran the whole gamut of attitudes available to one human being vis-à-vis another, from pure love to total indifference—"ghost" offers one more possibility, if you will, a postscript, a sum total. "Dear ghost" is uttered here indeed with an air of discovery and of summary, which is what, in fact, the poem offers two lines later: "Yet abides the fact, indeed, the same— / You are past love, praise, indifference, blame." This describes not only the condition of a ghost but also a new attitude attained by the poet—an attitude that permeates the cycle of *Poems from 1912–13* and without which that cycle wouldn't be possible.

This finale's enumeration of attitudes is tactically similar to "The Convergence of the Twain"'s "grotesque, slimed, dumb, indifferent." Yet while it is propelled by similar self-deprecating logic, it adds up not to the reductive ("choose one") precision of analysis but to an extraordinary emotional summary that redefines the genre of funeral elegy no less than that of love poetry itself. Immediate as the former, "Your Last Drive" amounts on account of its finale to a much-delayed postscript, rarely encountered in poetry, to what love amounts to. Such a summary is obviously the minimal requirement for engaging a ghost in a dialogue, and the last line has an engaging, indeed somewhat flirtatious air. Our old man is wooing the inanimate.

VII

Every poet learns from his own breakthroughs, and Hardy, with his professed tendency to "exact a full look at the worst," seems to profit in, and from, *Poems of 1912–13* enormously. For all its riches of detail and topographical reference, the cycle has an oddly universal, almost impersonal quality, since it deals with the extremes of the emotional spectrum. "A full look at the worst" is well matched by a full look at the best, with very short shrift given to the mean. It is as though a book were being riffled through from the end to the beginning before being shelved.

It never got shelved. A rationalist more than an emotionalist, Hardy, of course, saw the cycle as an opportunity to rectify what many and in part he himself regarded as a lyrical deficiency in his poetry. And true enough, *Poems of 1912–13* does constitute a considerable departure from his pattern of graveyard musing, grand on metaphysics and yet usually rather bland sentimentally. That's what accounts for the cycle's enterprising stanzaic architecture, but above all for its zeroing in on the initial stage of his marital union: on meeting a maiden.

In theory, that encounter ensures an upsurge of positive sentiment, and at times it does. But it was so long ago that the optic of intro- and retrospection often proves insufficient. As such it gets unwittingly replaced by the lens habitually employed by our poet for pondering his beloved infinities, Immanent Wills, and all, exacting a full look at the worst.

It seems he's got no other instruments anyway: whenever faced with a choice between a moving or a drastic utterance, he normally goes for the latter. This may be attributed to certain aspects of Mr. Hardy's character or temperament: a more appropriate attribution would be to the métier itself.

For poetry for Thomas Hardy was above all a tool of cognition. His correspondence as well as his prefaces to various editions of his work are full of disclaimers of a poetic vocation; they often emphasize the diaristic, commentary role his poetry had for him. I think this can be taken at face value. We should bear in mind also that the man was an autodidact, and autodidacts are always more interested in the substance of what they are learning than its actual data. When it comes to poetry, this boils down to an emphasis on revelatory capacity, often at the expense of harmony.

To be sure, Hardy went to extraordinary lengths to master harmony, and his craftsmanship often borders on the exemplary. Still, it is just craftsmanship. He is no genius at harmony; his lines seldom sing. The music available in his poems is a mental music, and as such it is absolutely unique. The main distinction of Thomas Hardy's verse is that its formal aspects—rhyme, meter, alliteration, etc.—are precisely the aspects standing in attendance to the driving force of his thought. In other words, they seldom generate that force; their main job is to usher in an idea and not to obstruct its progress.

I suppose if asked what he values more in a poem—the insight or the texture—he would cringe, but ultimately he would give the autodidact's reply: the insight. This is, then, the criterion by which one is to judge his work, and this cycle in particular. It is the extension of human insight that he sought in this study of the extremes of estrangement and attachment, rather than pure self-expression. In this sense, this pre-modernist was without peer. In this sense also, his poems are indeed a true reflection of the métier itself, whose operational mode, too, is the fusion of the rational and the intuitive. It could be said, however, that he turned the tables somewhat: he was intuitive about his work's substance; as for his verse's formal aspects, he was excessively rational.

For that he paid dearly. A good example of this could be his "In the Moonlight," written a couple of years later but in a sense belonging to *Poems of 1912–13*—if not necessarily thematically, then by virtue of its psychological vector.

> "O lonely workman, standing there
> In a dream, why do you stare and stare
> At her grave, as no other grave there were?

> "If your great gaunt eyes so importune
> Her soul by the shine of this corpse-cold moon
> Maybe you'll raise her phantom soon!"

> "Why, fool, it is what I would rather see
> Than all the living folk there be;
> But alas, there is no such joy for me!"

> "Ah—she was one you loved, no doubt,
> Through good and evil, through rain and drought,
> And when she passed, all your sun went out?"

> "Nay: she was the woman I did not love,
> Whom all the others were ranked above,
> Whom during her life I thought nothing of."

Like an extremely high percentage of Hardy's verse, the poem seems to hark back to the folk ballad, with its use of dialogue and its element of social commentary. The mock romantic opening and the nagging lapidary tone of triplets—not to mention the poem's very title—suggest a polemical aspect to "In the Moonlight" when viewed within the contemporary poetic discourse. The poem is obviously a "variation on a theme" frequent enough in Hardy's own work in the first place.

The overtones of social commentary, usually fairly sharp in a ballad, are somewhat muted here, though not entirely. Rather, they are subordinated to the psychological thrust of the poem. It is extremely shrewd of Hardy to make precisely a "workman," and not the urbane, sneering passerby the carrier of the loaded, terrifying insight revealed in the last stanza. For normally a crisis-ridden conscience in literature is the property of the educated classes. Here, however, it is an uncouth, almost plebeian "workman" who weighs in with at once the most menacing and the most tragic admission Hardy's verse ever made.

Yet although the syntax here is fairly clear, the meter sustained, and the psychology powerful, the poem's texture undermines its mental achievement with its triple rhyme, warranted neither by the story line nor, what's worse, its own quality. In short, the job is expert but not particularly rewarding. We get the poem's vector, not its target. But so far as the truth about the human heart is concerned, this vector may be enough. That's what the poet, one imagines, has told himself on this and on many other occasions. For the full look at the worst blinds you to your own appearance.

VIII

Blissfully, Hardy lived long enough not to be trapped by either his achievements or his failures. Therefore, we may concentrate on his achievements, perhaps with an additional sense of their humanity or, if you will, independent of it. Here's one of them, a poem called "Afterwards." It was written somewhere around 1917, when quite a lot of people all over the place were busy doing each other in and when our poet was seventy-seven years old.

When the Present has latched its postern behind my tremulous stay,
  And the May month flaps its glad green leaves like wings,
Delicate-filmed as new-spun silk, will the neighbours say,
  "He was a man who used to notice such things"?

If it be in the dusk when, like an eyelid's soundless blink,
  The dewfall-hawk comes crossing the shades to alight
Upon the wind-warped upland thorn, a gazer may think,
  "To him this must have been a familiar sight."

If I pass during some nocturnal blackness, mothy and warm,
  When the hedgehog travels furtively over the lawn.
One may say, "He strove that such innocent creatures should come to no harm,
  But he could do little for them; and now he is gone."

If, when hearing that I have been stilled at last, they stand at the door,
  Watching the full-starred heavens that winter sees,
Will this thought rise on those who will meet my face no more,
  "He was one who had an eye for such mysteries"?

And will any say when my bell of quittance is heard in the gloom,

> *And a crossing breeze cuts a pause in its outrollings,*
> *Till they rise again, as they were a new bell's boom,*
> * "He hears it not now, but used to notice such things"?*

These twenty hexametric lines are the glory of English poetry, and they owe all that they've got precisely to hexameter. The good question is to what does hexameter itself owe its appearance here, and the answer is so that the old man can breathe more easily. Hexameter is here not for its epic or by the same classical token elegiac connotations but for its trimeter-long, inhale-exhale properties. On the subconscious level, this comfort translates into the availability of time, into a generous margin. Hexameter, if you will, is a moment stretched, and with every next word Thomas Hardy in "Afterwards" stretches it even further.

The conceit in this poem is fairly simple: while considering his immanent passing, the poet produces cameo representations of each one of the four seasons as his departure's probable backdrop. Remarkably well served by its title and free of the emotional investment usually accompanying a poet when such prospects are entertained, the poem proceeds at a pace of melancholy meditation—which is what Mr. Hardy, one imagines, wanted it to be. It appears, however, that somewhere along the way the poem escaped his control and things began to occur in it not according to the initial plan. In other words, art has overtaken craft.

But first things first, and the first season here is spring, which is ushered in with an awkward, almost creaking septuagenarian elegance: no sooner does May get in than it is hit by a stress. This is all the more noticeable after the indeed highly arch and creaking "When the Present has latched its postern behind my tremulous stay," with its wonderfully hissing confluence of sibilants toward the end of the line. "Tremulous stay" is a splendid conjunction, evocative, one would imagine, of the poet's very voice at this stage, and thus setting the tone for the rest of the poem.

Of course, we have to bear in mind that we are viewing the whole thing through the prism of the modern, late-twentieth-century idiom in poetry. What seems arch and antiquated through this lens wouldn't necessarily have produced the same effect at the time. When it comes to generating circumlocutions, death has no equals, and at the Last Judgment it could cite them in its defense. And as such circumlocutions go, "When the Present has latched its postern behind my tremulous stay" is wonderful if only because it shows a poet more concerned with his diction than with the prospect he describes. There is a peace in this line, not least because the stressed words here are two and three syllables long; the unstressed syllables play the rest of these words down with the air of a postscript or an afterthought.

Actually, the stretching of the hexameter—i.e., time—and filling it up begins with "tremulous stay." But things really get busy once the stress hits "May" in the second line, which consists solely of monosyllables. Euphonically, the net result in the second line is an impression that Mr. Hardy's spring is more rich in leaf than any August. Psychologically, however, one has the sense of piling-up qualifiers spilling well into the third line, with its hyphenated, Homer-like epithets. The overall sensation (embodied in the future perfect tense) is that of time slowed down, stalled by its every second, for that's what monosyllabic words are: uttered—or printed—seconds.

"The best eye for natural detail," enthused Yvor Winters about Thomas Hardy. And we, of course, can admire this eye sharp enough to liken the reverse side of a leaf to newly spun silk—but only at the expense of praising the ear. As you read these lines out loud, you stumble through the second, and you've got to mumble fast through the first half of the third. And it occurs to you that the poet has stuffed these lines with so much natural detail not for its own sake but for reasons of metric vacancy.

The truth, of course, is that it's both: that's your real natural detail: the ratio of, say, a leaf to the amount of space in a line. It may fit, and then it may not. This is the way a poet learns the value of that leaf as well as of those available stresses. And it is to alleviate the syllabic density of the preceding line that Mr. Hardy produces the almost trochaic "Delicate-filmed as new-spun silk" qualifier, not out of attachment to this leaf and this particular sensation. Had he been attached to them, he'd have moved them to the rhyming position, or in any case out of the tonal limbo where you find them.

Still, technically speaking, this line and a half do show off what Mr. Winters appreciates so much about our poet. And our poet himself is cognizant of trotting out natural detail here, and polishing it up a bit on top of that. And this is what enables him to wrap it up with the colloquial "He was a man who used to notice such things." This understatement, nicely counterbalancing the opening line's ramshackle grandeur, is what he was perhaps after in the first place. It's highly quotable, so he attributes it to the neighbors, clearing the line of the charge of self-consciousness, let alone of being an autoepitaph.

There is no way for me to prove this—though there is also no way to refute it—but I think the first and last lines, "When the Present has latched its postern behind my tremulous stay" and "He was a man who used to notice such things," existed long before "Afterwards" was conceived, independently. Natural detail got in between them by chance, because it provided a rhyme (not a very spectacular one, so it needed a qualifier). Once there, it gave the poet a stanza, and with that came the pattern for the rest of the poem. These particular things, then, don't actually seem to be what he's noticing; it's the *idea* of noticing, in a particular way.

One indication of this is the uncertainty of the season in the next stanza. I'd suggest it's autumn, since the stanzas after deal respectively with summer and winter; and the leafless thorn seems fallow and chilled. This succession is slightly odd in Hardy, who is a superb plotter and who, you might think, would be one to handle the seasons in the traditional, orderly manner. That said, however, the second stanza is a work of unique beauty.

It all starts with yet another confluence of sibilants in "eyelid's soundless blink." Again, proving and refuting may be a problem, but I tend to think that "an eyelid's soundless blink" is a reference to Petrarch's "One life is shorter than an eyelid's blink"; "Afterwards," as we know, is a poem about one's demise.

But even if we abandon the first line with its magnificent caesura followed by those two rustling *s*'s between "eyelids" and "soundless," ending with two more *s*'s, we've got plenty here. First, we have this very cinematographic, slow-motion passage of "The dewfall-hawk" that "comes crossing the shades to alight..." And we have to pay attention to his choice of the word "shades," considering our subject. And if we do, we may further wonder about this "dewfall-hawk," about its "dewfall" bit especially. What, we may ask, does this "dewfall," following an eyelid's blink and preceding "shade," try to do here, and is it, perhaps, a well-buried tear? And don't we hear in "to alight / Upon the wind-warped upland thorn" a reined-in or overpowered emotion?

Perhaps we don't. Perhaps all we hear is a pile up of stresses, at best evoking through their "up / warp / up" sound the clapping of wind-pestered shrubs. Against such a backdrop, an impersonal, unreacting "gazer" would be an apt way to describe the onlooker, stripped of any human characteristics, reduced to eyesight. "Gazer" is fitting, since he observes our speaker's absence and thus can't be described in detail: probability can't be terribly particular. Similarly the hawk, batting its wings like eyelids through "the shades," is moving through the same absence. The refrainlike "To him this must have been a familiar sight" is all the more poignant because it cuts both ways: the hawk's flight here is as real as it is posthumous.

On the whole, the beauty of "Afterwards" is that everything in it is multiplied by two.

The next stanza considers, I believe, the summer, and the opening line overwhelms you with its tactility in "mothy and warm," all the more palpable because it is isolated by a very bravely shifted caesura. Yet speaking of bravery, it should be noted that only a very healthy person can ponder the nocturnal blackness of the moment of his demise with such equipoise as we find in "If I pass during some nocturnal blackness..." Not to mention more cavalier treatment of the caesura. The only mark of possible alarm here is the "some" before "nocturnal blackness." On the other hand, "some" is one of those readily available bricks a poet uses to save his meter.

Be that as it may, the real winner in this stanza is obviously "When the hedgehog travels furtively over the lawn"—and within the line itself it is, of course, "furtively." The rest is slightly less animated and certainly less interesting, since our poet is clearly bent on endearing himself to the public with his pro-animal sympathies. That's quite unnecessary, since, given the subject, the reader is on his side as it is. Also, if one wanted to be really hard-nosed here, one could query whether that hedgehog was indeed in harm's way. At this stage, however, nobody wants to quibble. But the poet himself seems to be aware of the insufficiency of the material here; so he saddles his hexameter with three additional syllables ("One may say")—partly because the awkwardness of speech, he believes, suggests geniality, partly to stretch the dying man's time—or the time he is remembered.

It is in the fourth, winter stanza that the poem confronts absence in earnest.

> *If, when hearing that I have been stilled at last, they stand at the door,*
>> *Watching the full-starred heavens that winter sees,*
> *Will this thought rise on those who will meet my face no more,*
>> *"He was one who had an eye for such mysteries"?*

To begin with, being "stilled at last" includes within its euphemistic reach the author taking leave of the poem, as well as the poem's previous stanza growing silent. This way the audience, more numerous than "the neighbors," "a gazer," or "one," is ushered here into the text and asked to play the role of "Watching the full-starred heavens that winter sees." This is an extraordinary line; the natural detail here is positively terrifying and practically prefigures Robert Frost. For winter indeed sees more "heavens," since in winter trees are naked and the air is clear. If these heavens are full-starred, it sees more stars. The line is an apotheosis of absence, yet Mr. Hardy seeks to aggravate it further with "Will this thought rise on those who will meet my face no more." "Rise" imparts to the presumably cold features of the "stilled at last" the temperature of the moon.

Behind all this there is, of course, an old trope about the souls of the dead residing on stars. Still, the optical literalness of this rendition is blinding. Apparently when you see a winter sky you see Thomas Hardy. That's the kind of mystery he had an eye for, in his lifetime.

He had an eye for something closer to the ground, too. As you read "Afterwards," you begin to notice the higher and higher position in the lines of each stanza of those who are to comment on him. From the bottom in the first, they climb to the top in the fifth. This could be a coincidence with anyone other than Hardy. We also have to watch their progression from "the neighbours" to "a gazer" to "one" to "they" to "any." None of these designations is particular, let alone endearing. Well, who are these people?

Before we get to that, let's learn something about "any" and what he expects from them.

> And will any say when my bell of quittance is heard in the gloom.
>> And a crossing breeze cuts a pause in its outrollings,
>> Till they rise again, as they were a new bell's boom,
>>> "He hears it not now, but used to notice such things"?

There is no particular season here, which means it's any time. It's any backdrop also, presumably a countryside, with a church in the fields, and its bell tolling. The observation described in the second and third lines is lovely but too common for our poet to claim any distinction for making it. It's his ability to describe it that "any" might refer to by saying in his absence, "He hears it not now, but used to notice such things." Also, "such things" is a sound: interrupted by wind yet returning anew. An interrupted but resuming sound could be regarded here, at the end of this autoelegy, as a self-referential metaphor, and not because the sound in question is that of a bell tolling for Thomas Hardy.

It is so because an interrupted yet resuming sound is, in fact, a metaphor for poetry: for a succession of poems emerging from under the same pen, for a succession of stanzas within one poem. It is a metaphor for "Afterwards" itself, with all its peregrination of stresses and suddenly halting caesuras. In this sense, the bell of quittance never stops—not Mr. Hardy's, anyway. And it doesn't stop as long as his "neighbors," "gazer," "one," "they," and "any" are us.

IX

Extraordinary claims for a dead poet are best made on the basis of his entire oeuvre; as we are perusing only some of Thomas Hardy's work, we may dodge the temptation. Suffice it to say that he is one of the very few poets who, under minimal scrutiny, easily escape the past. What helps his escape is obviously the content of his poems: they are simply extraordinarily interesting to read. And to reread, since their texture is very often pleasure-resistant. That was his whole gamble, and he won.

Out of the past there is only one route, and it takes you into the present. However, Hardy's poetry is not a very comfortable presence here. He is seldom taught, still less read. First, with respect to contents at least, he simply overshadows the bulk of poetry's subsequent achievement: a comparison renders too many a modern giant a simpleton. As for the general readership, his thirst for the inanimate comes off as unappealing and disconcerting. Rather than the general public's mental health, this bespeaks its mental diet.

As he escapes the past, and sits awkwardly in the present, one trains one's eye on the future as perhaps his more appropriate niche. It is possible, although the technological and demographic watershed we are witnessing would seem to obliterate any foresight or fantasy based on our own relatively coherent experience. Still, it is possible, and not only because the triumphant Immanent Will might decide to acknowledge, at the peak of its glory, its early champion.

It is possible because Thomas Hardy's poetry makes considerable inroads into what is the target of all cognition: inanimate matter. Our species embarked on this quest long ago, rightly suspecting that we share our own cellular mix-up with the stuff, and that should the truth about the world exist, it's bound to be nonhuman. Hardy is not an exception. What is exceptional about him, however, is the relentlessness of his pursuit, in the course of which his poems began to acquire certain impersonal traits of his very subject, especially tonally. That could be regarded, of course, as camouflage, like wearing fatigues in the trenches.

Like a new line of fashion that set a trend in English poetry in this century: the dispassionate posture became practically the norm, indifference a trope. Still, these were just side effects; I daresay he went after the inanimate—not for its jugular, since it has none, but for its diction.

Come to think of it, the expression "matter-of-fact" could well apply to his idiom, except that the emphasis would be on matter. His poems very often sound as if matter has acquired the power of speech as yet another aspect of its human disguise. Perhaps this was indeed the case with Thomas Hardy. But then it's only natural, because as somebody—most likely it was I—once said, language is the inanimate's first line of information about itself, released to the animate. Or, to put it more accurately, language is a diluted aspect of matter.

It is perhaps because his poems almost invariably (once they exceed sixteen lines) either display the inanimate's touch or else keep an eye on it that the future may carve for him a somewhat larger niche than he occupies in the present. To paraphrase "Afterwards" somewhat, he used to notice un-human things; hence his "eye for natural detail," and numerous tombstone musings. Whether the future will be able to comprehend the laws governing matter better than has been done thus far remains to be seen. But it doesn't seem to have much choice in acknowledging a greater degree of human affinity with the inanimate than literature and philosophical thought have been insisting on.

This is what enables one to see in a crystal ball unfamiliar multitudes in odd attire making a run on Hardy's collected works.

JOSEPH BRODSKY

Poems

❖❖

Hap

If but some vengeful god would call to me
From up the sky, and laugh: "Thou suffering thing,
Know that they sorrow is my ecstasy,
That thy love's loss is my hate's profiting!"

Then would I bear it, clench myself, and die,
Steeled by the sense of ire unmerited;
Half-eased in that a Powerfuller than I
Had willed and meted me the tears I shed.

But not so. How arrives it joy lies slain,
And why unblooms the best hope ever sown?
—Crass Casualty obstructs the sun and rain,
And dicing Time for gladness casts a moan. . . .
These purblind Doomsters had as readily strown
Blisses about my pilgrimage as pain.

Neutral Tones

We stood by a pond that winter day,
And the sun was white, as though chidden of God,
And a few leaves lay on the starving sod;
    —They had fallen from an ash, and were gray.

Your eyes on me were as eyes that rove
Over tedious riddles of years ago;
And some words played between us to and fro
    On which lost the more by our love.

The smile on your mouth was the deadest thing
Alive enough to have strength to die;
And a grin of bitterness swept thereby
    Like an ominous bird a-wing. . . .

Since then, keen lessons that love deceives,
And wrings with wrong, have shaped to me
Your face, and the God-curst sun, and a tree,
    And a pond edged with grayish leaves.

Leipzig

SCENE—*The Master-tradesmen's Parlour at the Old Ship Inn,*
        Casterbridge. Evening.

"Old Norbert with the flat blue cap—
   A German said to be—
Why let your pipe die on your lap,
   Your eyes blink absently?"

—"Ah!. . . Well, I had thought till my cheek was wet
   Of my mother—her voice and mien
When she used to sing and pirouette,
   And tap the tambourine

"To the march that yon street-fiddler plies:
   She told me 'twas the same
She'd heard from the trumpets, when the Allies
   Burst on her home like flame.

"My father was one of the German Hussars,
   My mother of Leipzig; but he,
Being quartered here, fetched her at close of the wars,
   And a Wessex lad reared me.

"And as I grew up, again and again
   She'd tell, after trilling that air,
Of her youth, and the battles on Leipzig plain
   And of all that was suffered there!. . .

"—'Twas a time of alarms. Three Chiefs-at-arms
   Combined them to crush One,
And by numbers' might, for in equal fight
   He stood the matched of none.

"Carl Schwarzenberg was of the plot,
   And Blücher, prompt and prow,
And Jean the Crown-Prince Bernadotte:
   Buonaparte was the foe.

"City and plain had felt his reign
   From the North to the Middle Sea,
And he'd now sat down in the noble town
   Of the King of Saxony.

"October's deep dew its wet gossamer threw
    Upon Leipzig's lawns, leaf-strewn,
Where lately each fair avenue
    Wrought shade for summer noon.

"To westward two dull rivers crept
    Through miles of marsh and slough,
Whereover a streak of whiteness swept—
    The Bridge of Lindenau.

"Hard by, in the City, the One, care-tossed,
    Sat pondering his shrunken power;
And without the walls the hemming host
    Waxed denser every hour.

"He had speech that night on the morrow's designs
    With his chiefs by the bivouac fire,
While the belt of flames from the enemy's lines
    Flamed nigher him yet and nigher.

"Three rockets then from the girdling trine
    Told, 'Ready!' As they rose
Their flashes seemed his Judgment-Sign
    For bleeding Europe's woes.

"'Twas seen how the French watch-fires that night
    Glowed still and steadily;
And the Three rejoiced, for they read in the sight
    That the One disdained to flee....

"—Five hundred guns began the affray
    On next day morn at nine;

Such mad and mangling cannon-play
    Had never torn human line.

"Around the town three battles beat,
    Contracting like a gin;
As nearer marched the million feet
    Of columns closing in.

"The first battle nighed on the low Southern side;
    The second by the Western way;
The nearing of the third on the North was heard;
    —The French held all at bay.

"Against the first band did the Emperor stand;
    Against the second stood Ney;
Marmont against the third gave the order-word:
    —Thus raged it throughout the day.

"Fifty thousand sturdy souls on those trampled plains and
        knolls,
    Who met the dawn hopefully,
And were lotted their shares in a quarrel not theirs,
    Dropt then in their agony.

"'O,' the old folks said, 'ye Preachers stern!
    O so-called Christian time!
When will men's swords to ploughshares turn?
    When come the promised prime?'...
"—The clash of horse and man which that day began,
    Closed not as evening wore;
And the morrow's armies, rear and van,
    Still mustered more and more.

"From the City towers the Confederate Powers
    Were eyed in glittering lines,
And up from the vast a murmuring passed
    As from a wood of pines.

"'Tis well to cover a feeble skill
    By numbers' might!' scoffed He;
'But give me a third of their strength, I'd fill
    Half Hell with their soldiery!'

"All that day raged the war they waged,
    And again dumb night held reign,
Save that ever upspread from the dank deathbed
    A miles-wide pant of pain.

"Hard had striven brave Ney, the true Bertrand,
    Victor, and Augereau,
Bold Poniatowski, and Lauriston,
    To stay their overthrow;

"But, as in the dream of one sick to death
    There comes a narrowing room
That pens him, body and limbs and breath,
    To wait a hideous doom,

"So to Napoleon, in the hush
    That held the town and towers
Through these dire nights, a creeping crush
    Seemed borne in with the hours.

"One road to the rearward, and but one,
    Did fitful Chance allow;

'Twas where the Pleiss' and Elster run—
    The Bridge of Lindenau.

"The nineteenth dawned. Down street and Platz
    The wasted French sank back,
Stretching long lines across the Flats
    And on the bridgeway track:

"When there surged on the sky an earthen wave,
    And stones, and men, as though
Some rebel churchyard crew updrave
    Their sepulchres from below.

"To Heaven is blown Bridge Lindenau;
    Wrecked regiments reel therefrom;
And rank and file in masses plough
    The sullen Elster-Strom.

"A gulf was Lindenau; and dead
    Were fifties, hundreds, tens;
And every current rippled red
    With Marshal's blood and men's.

"The smart Macdonald swam therein,
    And barely won the verge;
Bold Poniatowski plunged him in
    Never to re-emerge.

"Then stayed the strife. The remnants wound
    Their Rhineward way pell-mell;
And thus did Leipzig City sound
    An Empire's passing bell;

"While in cavalcade, with band and blade,
    Came Marshals, Princes, Kings;
And the town was theirs... Ay, as simple maid,
    My mother saw these things!

"And whenever those notes in the street begin
    I recall her, and that far scene,
And her acting of how the Allies marched in,
    And her tap of the tambourine!"

In a Wood

See "The Woodlanders"

Pale beech and pine so blue,
        Set in one clay,
Bough to bough cannot you
        Live out your day?
When the rains skim and skip,
Why mar sweet comradeship,
Blighting with poison-drip
        Neighbourly spray?

Heart-halt and spirit-lame,
        City-opprest,
Unto this wood I came
        As to a nest;
Dreaming that sylvan peace
Offered the harrowed ease—
Nature a soft release
        From men's unrest.

But, having entered in,
  Great growths and small
Show them to men akin—
  Combatants all!
Sycamore shoulders oak,
Bines the slim sapling yoke,
Ivy-spun halters choke
  Elms stout and tall.

Touches from ash, O wych,
  Sting you like scorn!
You, too, brave hollies, twitch
  Sidelong from thorn.
Even the rank poplars bear
Lothly a rival's air,
Cankering in black despair
  If overborne.

Since, then, no grace I find
  Taught me of trees,
Turn I back to my kind,
  Worthy as these.
There at least smiles abound,
There discourse trills around,
There, now and then, are found
  Life-loyalties.
1887: 1896

I Look into My Glass

I look into my glass,

And view my wasting skin,
And say, "Would God it came to pass
My heart had shrunk as thin!"

For then, I, undistrest
By hearts grown cold to me,
Could lonely wait my endless rest
With equanimity.

But Time, to make me grieve,
Part steals, lets part abide;
And shakes this fragile frame at eve
With throbbings of noontide.

Drummer Hodge

I

They throw in Drummer Hodge, to rest
    Uncoffined—just as found:
His landmark is a kopje-crest
    That breaks the veldt around;
And foreign constellations west
    Each night above his mound.

II

Young Hodge the Drummer never knew—
    Fresh from his Wessex home—
The meaning of the broad Karoo,
    The Bush, the dusty loam,

And why uprose to nightly view
    Strange stars amid the gloom.

III

Yet portion of that unknown plain
    Will Hodge for ever be;
His homely Northern breast and brain
    Grow to some Southern tree,
And strange-eyed constellations reign
    His stars eternally.

The Souls of the Slain

I

The thick lids of Night closed upon me
    Alone at the Bill
    Of the Isle by the Race—
Many-caverned, bald, wrinkled of face—
And with darkness and silence the spirit was on me
    To brood and be still.

II

No wind fanned the flats of the ocean,
    Or promontory sides,
    Or the ooze by the strand,
    Or the bent-bearded slope of the land,
Whose base took its rest amid everlong motion
    Of criss-crossing tides.

III

Soon from out of the Southward seemed nearing
　　A whirr, as of wings
　　Waved by mighty-vanned flies,
　Or by night-moths of measureless size,
And in softness and smoothness well-nigh beyond hearing
　　Of corporal things.

IV

And they bore to the bluff, and alighted—
　　A dim-discerned train
　　Of sprites without mould,
　Frameless souls none might touch or might hold—
On the ledge by the turreted lantern, far-sighted
　　By men of the main.

V

And I heard them say "Home!" and I knew them
　　For souls of the felled
　　On the earth's nether bord
　Under Capricorn, whither they'd warred,
And I neared in my awe, and gave heedfulness to them
　　With breathings inheld.

VI

Then, it seemed, there approached from the northward
　　A senior soul-flame
　　Of the like filmy hue:

And he met them and spake: "Is it you,
O my men?" Said they, "Aye! We bear homeward and
    hearthward
      To feast on our fame!"

VII

"I've flown there before you," he said then:
    "Your households are well;
    But—your kin linger less
On your glory and war-mightiness
Than on dearer things."—"Dearer?" cried these from the dead
    then,
      "Of what do they tell?"

VIII

"Some mothers muse sadly, and murmur
    Your doings as boys—
    Recall the quaint ways
Of your babyhood's innocent days.
Some pray that, ere dying, your faith had grown firmer,
    And higher your joys.

IX

"A father broods: 'Would I had set him
    To some humble trade,
    And so slacked his high fire,
And his passionate martial desire;
And told him no stories to woo him and whet him
    To this dire crusade!'"

X

"And, General, how hold out our sweethearts,
　　Sworn loyal as doves?"
　　—"Many mourn; many think
　　It is not unattractive to prink
Them in sables for heroes. Some fickle and fleet hearts
　　Have found them new loves."

XI

"And our wives?" quoth another resignedly,
　　"Dwell they on our deeds?"
　　—"Deeds of home; that live yet
Fresh as new—deeds of fondness or fret;
Ancient words that were kindly expressed or unkindly,
　　These, these have their heeds."

XII

—"Alas! then it seems that our glory
　　Weighs less in their thought
　　Than our old homely acts,
　　And the long-ago commonplace facts
Of our lives—held by us as scarce part of our story,
　　And rated as nought!"

XIII

Then bitterly some: "Was it wise now
　　To raise the tomb-door
　　For such knowledge? Away!"

But the rest: "Fame we prized till to-day;
Yet that hearts keep us green for old kindness we prize now
    A thousand times more!"

XIV

Thus speaking, the trooped apparitions
    Began to disband
    And resolve them in two:
Those whose record was lovely and true
Bore to northward for home: those of bitter traditions
    Again left the land,

XV

And, towering to seaward in legions,
    They paused at a spot
    Overbending the Race—
That engulphing, ghast, sinister place—
Whither headlong they plunged, to the fathomless regions
    Of myriads forgot.

XVI

And the spirits of those who were homing
    Passed on, rushingly,
    Like the Pentecost Wind;
And the whirr of their wayfaring thinned
And surceased on the sky, and but left in the gloaming
    Sea-mutterings and me.

Shelley's Skylark

The neighbourhood of Leghorn: March 1887

Somewhere afield here something lies
In Earth's oblivious eyeless trust
That moved a poet to prophecies—
A pinch of unseen, unguarded dust:

The dust of the lark that Shelley heard,
And made immortal through times to be;—
Though it only lived like another bird,
And knew not its immortality:

Lived its meek life; then, one day, fell—
A little ball of feather and bone;
And how it perished, when piped farewell,
And where it wastes, are alike unknown.

Maybe it rests in the loam I view,
Maybe it throbs in a myrtle's green,
Maybe it sleeps in the coming hue
Of a grape on the slopes of yon inland scene.

Go find it, faeries, go and find
That tiny pinch of priceless dust,
And bring a casket silver-lined,
And framed of gold that gems encrust;

And we will lay it safe therein,
And consecrate it to endless time;
For it inspired a bard to win
Ecstatic heights in thought and rhyme.

Rome
At the Pyramid of Cestius near the
Graves of Shelley and Keats

Who, then, was Cestius,
And what is he to me?—
Amid thick thoughts and memories multitudinous
One thought alone brings he.

I can recall no word
Of anything he did;
For me he is a man who died and was interred
To leave a pyramid

Whose purpose was exprest
Not with its first design,
Nor till, far down in Time, beside it found their rest
Two countrymen of mine.

Cestius in life, maybe,
Slew, breathed out threatening;
I know not. This I know: in death all silently
He does a finer thing.

In beckoning pilgrim feet
With marble finger high
To where, by shadowy wall and history-haunted street,
Those matchless singers lie....

—Say, then, he lived and died
That stones which bear his name
Should mark, through Time, where two immortal Shades
    abide;
It is an ample fame.

On an Invitation to the United States

I

My ardours for emprize nigh lost
Since Life has bared its bones to me,
I shrink to seek a modern coast
Whose riper times have yet to be;
Where the new regions claim them free
From that long drip of human tears
Which peoples old in tragedy
Have left upon the centuried years.

II

For, wonning in these ancient lands,
Enchased and lettered as a tomb,
And scored with prints of perished hands,
And chronicled with dates of doom,
Though my own Being bear no bloom
I trace the lives such scenes enshrine,
Give past exemplars present room,
And their experience count as mine.

I Said to Love

I said to Love,
"It is not now as in old days
When men adored thee and thy ways
All else above;

Named thee the Boy, the Bright, the One
Who spread a heaven beneath the sun,"
      I said to Love.

      I said to him,
"We now know more of thee than then;
We were but weak in judgment when,
      With hearts abrim,
We clamoured thee that thou would'st please
Inflict on us thine agonies,"
      I said to him.

      I said to Love,
"Thou art not young, thou art not fair,
No elfin darts, no cherub air,
      Nor swan, nor dove
Are thine; but features pitiless,
And iron daggers of distress,"
      I said to Love.

      "Depart then, Love!...
—Man's race shall perish, threatenest thou,
Without thy kindling coupling-vow?
The age to come the man of now
      Know nothing of?—
We fear not such a threat from thee;
We are too old in apathy!
Mankind shall cease,—So let it be,"
      I said to Love.

At a Lunar Eclipse

Thy shadow, Earth, from Pole to Central Sea,
Now steals along upon the Moon's meek shine
In even monochrome and curving line
Of imperturbable serenity.

How shall I link such sun-cast symmetry
With the torn troubled form I know as thine,
That profile, placid as a brow divine,
With continents of moil and misery?

And can immense Mortality but throw
So small a shade, and Heaven's high human scheme
Be hemmed within the coasts yon arc implies?

Is such the stellar gauge of earthly show,
Nation at war with nation, brains that teem,
Heroes, and women fairer than the skies?

The Subalterns

I

"Poor wanderer," said the leaden sky,
  "I fain would lighten thee,
But there are laws in force on high
  Which say it must not be."

II

—"It would not freeze thee, shorn one," cried
    The North, "knew I but how
To warm my breath, to slack my stride;
    But I am ruled as thou."

III

—"To-morrow I attack thee, wight,"
    Said Sickness, "Yet I swear
I bear thy little ark no spite,
    But am bid enter there."

IV

—"Come hither, Son," I heard Death say;
    "I did not will a grave
Should end thy pilgrimage to-day,
    But I, too, am a slave!"

V

We smiled upon each other then,
    And life to me had less
Of that fell look it wore ere when
    They owned their passiveness.

Mute Opinion

I

I traversed a dominion
Whose spokesmen spake out strong
Their purpose and opinion
Through pulpit, press, and song.
I scarce had means to note there
A large-eyed few, and dumb,
Who thought not as those thought there
That stirred the heat and hum.

II

When, grown a Shade, beholding
That land in lifetime trode,
To learn if its unfolding
Fulfilled its clamoured code,
I saw, in web unbroken,
Its history outwrought
Not as the loud had spoken,
But as the mute had thought.

To Flowers from Italy in Winter

Sunned in the South, and here to-day;
   —If all organic things
Be sentient, Flowers, as some men say,
   What are your ponderings?

How can you stay, nor vanish quite
    From this bleak spot of thorn,
And birch, and fir, and frozen white
    Expanse of the forlorn?

Frail luckless exiles hither brought!
    Your dust will not regain
Old sunny haunts of Classic thought
    When you shall waste and wane;

But mix with alien earth, be lit
    With frigid Boreal flame,
And not a sign remain in it
    To tell man whence you came.

To Lizbie Browne

I

Dear Lizbie Browne,
Where are you now?
In sun, in rain?—
Or is your brow
Past joy, past pain,
Dear Lizbie Browne?

II

Sweet Lizbie Browne,
How you could smile,
How you could sing!—

How archly wile
In glance-giving,
Sweet Lizbie Browne!

III

And, Lizbie Browne,
Who else had hair
Bay-red as yours,
Or flesh so fair
Bred out of doors,
Sweet Lizbie Browne?

IV

When, Lizbie Browne,
You had just begun
To be endeared
By stealth to one,
You disappeared
My Lizbie Browne!

V

Ay, Lizbie Browne,
So swift your life,
And mine so slow,
You were a wife
Ere I could show
Love, Lizbie Browne.

VI

Still, Lizbie Browne,
You won, they said,
The best of men
When you were wed. . . .
Where went you then,
O Lizbie Browne?

VII

Dear Lizbie Browne,
I should have thought,
"Girls ripen fast,"
And coaxed and caught
You ere you passed,
Dear Lizbie Browne!

VIII

But, Lizbie Browne,
I let you slip;
Shaped not a sign;
Touched never your lip
With lip of mine,
Lost Lizbie Browne!

IX

So, Lizbie Browne,
When on a day
Men speak of me

As not, you'll say,
"And who was he?"—
Yes, Lizbie Browne!

A Broken Appointment

You did not come,
And marching Time drew on, and wore me numb.—
Yet less for loss of your dear presence there
Than that I thus found lacking in your make
That high compassion which can overbear
Reluctance for pure lovingkindness' sake
Grieved I, when, as the hope-hour stroked its sum,
You did not come.

You love not me,
And love alone can lend you loyalty;
—I know and knew it. But, unto the store
Of human deeds divine in all but name,
Was it not worth a little hour or more
To add yet this: Once you, a woman, came
To soothe a time-torn man; even though it be
You love not me?

The Widow Betrothed

I passed the lodge and avenue
    To her fair tenement,
And sunset on her window-panes
    Reflected our intent.

The creeper on the gable nigh
    Was fired to more than red,
And when I came to halt thereby
    "Bright as my joy!" I said.

Of late days it had been her aim
    To meet me in the hall;
Now at my footsteps no one came,
    And no one to my call.

Again I knocked, and tardily
    An inner tread was heard,
And I was shown her presence then
    With a mere answering word.

She met me, and but barely took
    My proffered warm embrace;
Preoccupation weighed her look,
    And hardened her sweet face.

"To-morrow—could you—would you call?
    Abridge your present stay?
My child is ill—my one, my all!—
    And can't be left to-day."

And then she turns, and gives commands
    As I were out of sound,
Or were no more to her and hers
    Than any neighbour round. . . .

—As maid I loved her; but one came
    And pleased, and coaxed, and wooed,

And when in time he wedded her
　　I deemed her gone for good.

He won, I lost her; and my loss
　　I bore I know not how;
But I do think I suffered then
　　Less wretchedness than now.

For Time, in taking him, unclosed
　　An unexpected door
Of bliss for me, which grew to seem
　　Far surer than before.

Yet in my haste I overlooked
　　When secondly I sued
That then, as not at first, she had learnt
　　The call of motherhood. . . .

Her word is steadfast, and I know
　　How firmly pledged are we:
But a new love-claim shares her since
　　She smiled as maid on me!

The Darkling Thrush

I leant upon a coppice gate
　　When Frost was spectre-gray,
And Winter's dregs made desolate
　　The weakening eye of day.
The tangled bine-stems scored the sky
　　Like strings of broken lyres,

And all mankind that haunted nigh
    Had sought their household fires.

The land's sharp features seemed to be
    The Century's corpse outleant,
His crypt the cloudy canopy,
    The wind his death-lament.
The ancient pulse of germ and birth
    Was shrunken hard and dry,
And every spirit upon earth
    Seemed fervourless as I.

At once a voice arose among
    The bleak twigs overhead
In a full-hearted evensong
    Of joy illimited;
An aged thrush, frail, gaunt, and small,
    In blast-beruffled plume,
Had chosen thus to fling his soul
    Upon the growing gloom.

So little cause for carolings
    Of such ecstatic sound
Was written on terrestrial things
    Afar or nigh around,
That I could think there trembled through
    His happy good-night air
Some blessed Hope, whereof he knew
    And I was unaware.

The Comet at Yell'ham

I

It bends far over Yell'ham Plain,
    And we, from Yell'ham Height,
Stand and regard its fiery train,
    So soon to swim from sight.

II

It will return long years hence, when
    As now its strange swift shine
Will fall on Yell'ham; but not then
    On that sweet form of thine.

The Ruined Maid

"O 'melia, my dear, this does everything crown!
Who could have supposed I should meet you in Town?
And whence such fair garments, such prosperi-ty?"—
"O didn't you know I'd been ruined?" said she.

—"You left us in tatters, without shoes or socks,
Tired of digging potatoes, and spudding up docks;
And now you've gay bracelets and bright feathers three!"—
"Yes: that's how we dress when we're ruined," said she.

—"At home in the barton you said 'thee' and 'thou,'
And 'thik oon', and 'theäs oon', and 't'other'; but now
Your talking quite fits 'ee for high compa-ny!"—
"Some polish is gained with one's ruin," said she.

—"Your hands were like paws then, your face blue and bleak
But now I'm bewitched by your delicate cheek,
And your little gloves fit as on any la-dy!"—
"We never do work when we're ruined," said she.

—"You used to call home-life a hag-ridden dream,
And you'd sigh, and you'd sock; but at present you seem
To know not of megrims or melancho-ly!"—
"True. One's pretty lively when ruined," said she.

—"I wish I had feathers, a fine sweeping gown,
And a delicate face, and could strut about Town!"—
"My dear—a raw country girl, such as you be,
Cannot quite expect that. You ain't ruined," said she.

Westbourne Park Villas, 1866

In Tenebris I

Percussus sum sicut fœnum, et aruit cor meum.—Ps. CI

Wintertime nighs;
But my bereavement-pain
It cannot bring again:
Twice no one dies.

Flower-petals flee;
But, since it once hath been,
No more that severing scene
Can harrow me.

Birds faint in dread:
I shall not lose old strength
In the lone frost's black length:
Strength long since fled!

Leaves freeze to dun;
But friends can not turn cold
This season as of old
For him with none.

Tempests may scath;
But love can not make smart
Again this year his heart
Who no heart hath.

Black is night's cope;
But death will not appal
One who, past doubtings all,
Waits in unhope.

In Tenebris II

Considerabam ad dexteram, et videbam; et non erat qui cognosceret me. . . . non est
qui requirat animam meam.—Ps. CXLI

When the clouds' swoln bosoms echo back the shouts of the
many and strong
That things are all as they best may be, save a few to be right
ere long,
And my eyes have not the vision in them to discern what to
these is so clear,

The blot seems straightway in me alone; one better he were
not here.

The stout upstanders say, All's well with us: ruers have
nought to rue!
And what the potent say so oft, can it fail to be somewhat
true?
Breezily go they, breezily come; their dust smokes around
their career,
Till I think I am one born out of due time, who has no calling
here.

Their dawns bring lusty joys, it seems; their evenings all that
is sweet;
Our times are blessed times, they cry: Life shapes it as is most
meet,
And nothing is much the matter; there are many smiles to a
tear;
Then what is the matter is I, I say. Why should such an one
be here? . . .

Let him in whose ears the low-voiced Best is killed by the
clash of the First,
Who holds that if way to the Better there be, it exacts a full
look at the Worst,
Who feels that delight is a delicate growth cramped by
crookedness, custom, and fear,
Get him up and be gone as one shaped awry; he disturbs the
order here.

The Church-Builder

I

The church flings forth a battled shade
 Over the moon-blanched sward;
The church; my gift; whereto I paid
 My all in hand and hoard;
  Lavished my gains
  With stintless pains
To glorify the Lord.

II

I squared the broad foundations in
 Of ashlared masonry;
I moulded mullions thick and thin,
 Hewed fillet and ogee:
  I circleted
  Each sculptured head
With nimb and canopy.

III

I called in many a craftsmaster
 To fix emblazoned glass,
To figure Cross and Sepulchre
 On dossal, boss, and brass.
  My gold all spent,
  My jewels went
To gem the cups of Mass.

IV

I borrowed deep to carve the screen
    And raise the ivoried Rood;
I parted with my small demesne
    To make my owings good.
      Heir-looms unpriced
      I sacrificed,
    Until debt-free I stood.

V

So closed the task. "Deathless the Creed
    Here substanced!" said my soul:
"I heard me bidden to this deed,
    And straight obeyed the call.
      Illume this fane,
      That not in vain
    I build it, Lord of all!"

VI

But, as it chanced me, then and there
    Did dire misfortunes burst;
My home went waste for lack of care,
    My sons rebelled and curst;
      Till I confessed
      That aims the best
    Were looking like the worst.

VII

Enkindled by my votive work
    No burning faith I find;
The deeper thinkers sneer and smirk,
    And give my toil no mind;
        From nod and wink
        I read they think
That I am fool and blind.

VIII

My gift to God seems futile, quite;
    The world moves as erstwhile;
And powerful Wrong on feeble Right
    Tramples in olden style.
        My faith burns down,
        I see no crown;
But Cares, and Griefs, and Guile.

IX

So now, the remedy? Yea, this:
    I gently swing the door
Here, of my fane—no soul to wis—
    And cross the patterned floor
        To the rood-screen
        That stands between
The nave and inner chore.

X

The rich red windows dim the moon,
    But little light need I;
I mount the prie-dieu, lately hewn
    From woods of rarest dye;
      Then from below
      My garment, so,
I draw this cord, and tie

XI

One end thereof around the beam
    Midway 'twixt Cross and truss:
I noose the nethermost extreme,
    And in ten seconds thus
      I journey hence—
      To that land whence
No rumour reaches us.

XII

Well: Here at morn they'll light on one
    Dangling in mockery
Of what he spent his substance on
    Blindly and uselessly!...
      "He might," they'll say,
      "Have built, some way,
A cheaper gallows-tree!"

Shut Out That Moon

Close up the casement, draw the blind,
    Shut out that stealing moon,
She wears too much the guise she wore
    Before our lutes were strewn
With years-deep dust, and names we read
    On a white stone were hewn.

Step not forth on the dew-dashed lawn
    To view the Lady's Chair,
Immense Orion's glittering form,
    The Less and Greater Bear:
Stay in; to such sights we were drawn
    When faded ones were fair.

Brush not the bough for midnight scents
    That come forth lingeringly,
And wake the same sweet sentiments
    They breathed to you and me
When living seemed a laugh, and love
    All it was said to be.

Within the common lamp-lit room
    Prison my eyes and thought;
Let dingy details crudely loom,
    Mechanic speech be wrought:
Too fragrant was Life's early bloom,
    Too tart the fruit it brought!

LOVE LYRICS

1967

In five-score summers! All new eyes,
New minds, new modes, new fools, new wise;
New woes to weep, new joys to prize;

With nothing left of me and you
In that live century's vivid view
Beyond a pinch of dust or two;

A century which, if not sublime,
Will show, I doubt not, at its prime,
A scope above this blinkered time.

—Yet what to me how far above?
For I would only ask thereof
That thy worm should be my worm, Love!

On the Departure Platform

We kissed at the barrier; and passing through
She left me, and moment by moment got
Smaller and smaller, until to my view
  She was but a spot;

A wee white spot of muslin fluff
That down the diminishing platform bore
Through hustling crowds of gentle and rough
  To the carriage door.

Under the lamplight's fitful glowers,
Behind dark groups from far and near,
Whose interests were apart from ours,
    She would disappear,

Then show again, till I ceased to see
That flexible form, that nebulous white;
And she who was more than my life to me
    Had vanished quite. . . .

We have penned new plans since that fair fond day,
And in season she will appear again—
Perhaps in the same soft white array—
    But never as then!

—"And why, young man, must eternally fly
A joy you'll repeat, if you love her well?"
—O friend, nought happens twice thus; why,
    I cannot tell!

In a Cathedral City

These people have not heard your name;
No loungers in this placid place
Have helped to bruit your beauty's fame.

The grey Cathedral, towards whose face
Bend eyes untold, has met not yours;
Your shade has never swept its base,

Your form has never darked its doors,
Nor have your faultless feet once thrown
A pensive pit-pat on its floors.

Along the street to maids well known
Blithe lovers hum their tender airs,
But in your praise voice not a tone. . . .

—Since nought bespeaks you here, or bears,
As I, your imprint through and through,
Here might I rest, till my heart shares
The spot's unconsciousness of you!

Let Me Enjoy

Minor key

I

Let me enjoy the earth no less
Because the all-enacting Might
That fashioned forth its loveliness
Had other aims than my delight.

II

About my path there flits a Fair,
Who throws me not a word or sign;
I'll charm me with her ignoring air,
And laud the lips not meant for mine.

III

From manuscripts of moving song
Inspired by scenes and dreams unknown
I'll pour out raptures that belong
To others, as they were my own.

IV

And some day hence, toward Paradise
And all its blest—if such should be—
I will lift glad, afar-off eyes,
Though it contains no place for me.

At Casterbridge Fair

I. The Ballad-Singer

Sing, Ballad-singer, raise a hearty tune;
Make me forget that there was ever a one
I walked with in the meek light of the moon
    When the day's work was done.

Rhyme, Ballad-rhymer, start a country song;
Make me forget that she whom I loved well
Swore she would love me dearly, love me long,
    Then—what I cannot tell!

Sing, Ballad-singer, from your little book;
Make me forget those heart-breaks, achings, fears;

Make me forget her name, her sweet sweet look—
    Make me forget her tears.

II. *Former Beauties*

These market-dames, mid-aged, with lips thin-drawn,
    And tissues sere,
Are they the ones we loved in years agone,
    And courted here?

Are these the muslined pink young things to whom
    We vowed and swore
In nooks on summer Sundays by the Froom,
    Or Budmouth shore?

Do they remember those gay tunes we trod
    Clasped on the green;
Aye; trod till moonlight set on the beaten sod
    A satin sheen?

They must forget, forget! They cannot know
    What once they were,
Or memory would transfigure them, and show
    Them always fair.

III. *After the Club-Dance*

    Black'on frowns east on Maidon,
        And westward to the sea,
    But on neither is his frown laden
        With scorn, as his frown on me!

At dawn my heart grew heavy,
  I could not sip the wine,
I left the jocund bevy
  And that young man o' mine.

The roadside elms pass by me,—
  Why do I sink with shame
When the birds a-perch there eye me?
  They, too, have done the same!

IV. *The Market Girl*

Nobody took any notice of her as she stood on the causey
kerb,
All eager to sell her honey and apples and bunches of garden
herb;
And if she had offered to give her wares and herself with them
too that day,
I doubt if a soul would have cared to take a bargain so choice
away.

But chancing to trace her sunburnt grace that morning as I
passed nigh,
I went and I said "Poor maidy dear!—and will none of these
people buy?"
And so it began; and soon we knew what the end of it all
must be,
And I found that though no others had bid, a prize had been
won by me.

v. *The Inquiry*

And are ye one of Hermitage—
Of Hermitage, by Ivel Road,
And do ye know, in Hermitage
A thatch-roofed house where sengreens grow?
And does John Waywood live there still—
He of the name that there abode
When father hurdled on the hill
      Some fifteen years ago?

Does he now speak of o' Patty Beech,
The Patty Beech he used to—see,
Or ask at all if Patty Beech
Is known or heard of out this way?
—Ask ever if she's living yet,
And where her present home may be,
And how she bears life's fag and fret
      After so long a day?

In years agone at Hermitage
This faded face was counted fair,
None fairer; and at Hermitage
We swore to wed when he should thrive.
But never a chance had he or I,
And waiting made his wish outwear,
And Time, that dooms man's love to die,
      Preserves a maid's alive.

VI. *A Wife Waits*

Will's at the dance in the Club-room below,
    Where the tall liquor-cups foam;
I on the pavement up here by the Bow,
    Wait, wait, to steady him home.

Will and his partner are treading a tune,
    Loving companions they be;
Willy, before we were married in June,
    Said he loved no one but me;

Said he would let his old pleasures all go
    Ever to live with his Dear.
Will's at the dance in the Club-room below,
    Shivering I wait for him here.

VII. *After the Fair*

The singers are gone from the Cornmarket-place
    With their broadsheets of rhymes,
The street rings no longer in treble and bass
    With their skits on the times,
And the Cross, lately thronged, is a dim naked space
    That but echoes the stammering chimes.

From Clock-corner steps, as each quarter ding-dongs,
    Away the folk roam
By the "Hart" and Grey's Bridge into byways and "drongs",
    Or across the ridged loam;
The younger ones shrilling the lately heard songs,
    The old saying, "Would we were home."

| 112 |

The shy–seeming maiden so mute in the fair
    Now rattles and talks,
And that one who looked the most swaggering there
    Grows sad as she walks,
And she who seemed eaten by cankering care
    In statuesque sturdiness stalks.

And midnight clears High Street of all but the ghosts
    Of its buried burghees,
From the latest far back to those old Roman hosts
    Whose remains one yet sees,
Who loved, laughed, and fought, hailed their friends, drank
their toasts
    At their meeting-times here, just as these!

The Roman Road

        The Roman Road runs straight and bare
        As the pale parting-line in hair
        Across the heath. And thoughtful men
        Contrast its days of Now and Then,
        And delve, and measure, and compare;
        Visioning on the vacant air
        Helmed legionaries, who proudly rear
        The Eagle, as they pace again
                        The Roman Road.

        But no tall brass-helmed legionnaire
        Haunts it for me. Uprises there
        A mother's form upon my ken,

Guiding my infant steps, as when
We walked that ancient thoroughfare,
                        The Roman Road.

The Reminder

While I watch the Christmas blaze
Paint the room with ruddy rays,
Something makes my vision glide
To the frosty scene outside.

There, to reach a rotting berry,
Toils a thrush,—constrained to very
Dregs of food by sharp distress,
Taking such with thankfulness.

Why, O starving bird, when I
One day's joy would justify,
And put misery out of view,
Do you make me notice you!

The Rambler

I do not see the hills around,
Nor mark the tints the copses wear;
I do not note the grassy ground
And constellated daisies there.

I hear not the contralto note
Of cuckoos hid on either hand,
The whirr that shakes the nighthawk's throat
When eve's brown awning hoods the land.

Some say each songster, tree, and mead—
All eloquent of love divine—
Receives their constant careful heed:
Such keen appraisement is not mine.

The tones around me that I hear,
The aspects, meanings, shapes I see,
Are those far back ones missed when near,
And now perceived too late by me!

In Front of the Landscape

Plunging and laboring on in a tide of visions,
        Dolorous and dear,
Forward I pushed my way as amid waste waters
        Stretching around,
Through whose eddies there glimmered the customed
landscape
        Yonder and near

Blotted to feeble mist. And the coomb and the upland
    Coppice-crowned,
Ancient chalk-pit, milestone, rills in the grass-flat
    Stroked by the light,
Seemed but a ghost-like gauze, and no substantial
    Meadow or mound.

What were the infinite spectacles featuring foremost
    Under my sight,
Hindering me to discern my paced advancement
    Lengthening to miles;
What were the re-creations killing the daytime
    As by the night?

O they were speechful faces, gazing insistent,
    Some as with smiles,
Some as with slow-born tears that brinily trundled
    Over the wrecked
Cheeks that were fair in their flush-time, ash now with
anguish,
    Harrowed by wiles.

Yes, I could see them, feel them, hear them, address them—
    Halo-bedecked—
And, alas, onwards, shaken by fierce unreason,
    Rigid in hate,
Smitten by years-long wryness born of misprision,
    Dreaded, suspect.

Then there would breast me shining sights, sweet seasons
    Further in date;
Instruments of strings with the tenderest passion
    Vibrant, beside

Lamps long extinguished, robes, cheeks, eyes with the earth's
crust
     Now corporate.

Also there rose a headland of hoary aspect
     Gnawed by the tide,
Frilled by the nimb of the morning as two friends stood there
     Guilelessly glad—
Wherefore they knew not—touched by the fringe of an ecstasy
     Scantly descried.

Later images too did the day unfurl me,
     Shadowed and sad,
Clay cadavers of those who had shared in the dramas,
     Laid now at ease,
Passions all spent, chiefest the one of the broad brow
     Sepulture-clad.

So did beset me scenes, miscalled of the bygone,
     Over the leaze,
Past the clump, and down to where lay the beheld ones;
     —Yea, as the rhyme
Sung by the sea-swell, so in their pleading dumbness
     Captured me these.

For, their lost revisiting manifestations
     In their live time
Much had I slighted, caring not for their purport,
     Seeing behind
Things more coveted, reckoned the better worth calling
     Sweet, sad, sublime.

| 117 |

Thus do they now show hourly before the intenser
        Stare of the mind
As they were ghosts avenging their slights by my bypast
        Body-borne eyes,
Show, too, with fuller translation than rested upon them
        As living kind.

Hence wag the tongues of the passing people, saying
        In their surmise,
"Ah—whose is this dull form that perambulates, seeing
nought
        Round him that looms
Whithersoever his footsteps turn in his farings,
        Save a few tombs?"

The Convergence of the Twain

Lines on the loss of the "Titanic"

I

        In a solitude of the sea
        Deep from human vanity,
And the Pride of Life that planned her, stilly couches she.

II

        Steel chambers, late the pyres
        Of her salamandrine fires,
Cold currents thrid, and turn to rhythmic tidal lyres.

III

Over the mirrors meant
    To glass the opulent
The sea-worm crawls—grotesque, slimed, dumb, indifferent.

IV

Jewels in joy designed
    To ravish the sensuous mind
Lie lightless, all their sparkles bleared and black and blind.

V

Dim moon-eyed fishes near
    Gaze at the gilded gear
And query: "What does this vaingloriousness down here?"

VI

Well: while was fashioning
    This creature of cleaving wing,
The Immanent Will that stirs and urges everything

VII

Prepared a sinister mate
    For her—so gaily great—
A Shape of Ice, for the time far and dissociate.

VIII

And as the smart ship grew
In stature, grace, and hue
In shadowy silent distance grew the Iceberg too.

IX

Alien they seemed to be:
No mortal eye could see
The intimate welding of their later history,

X

Or sign that they were bent
By paths coincident
On being anon twin halves of one august event,

XI

Till the Spinner of the Years
Said "Now!" And each one hears,
And consummation comes, and jars two hemispheres.

Wessex Heights

There are some heights in Wessex, shaped as if by a kindly
hand
For thinking, dreaming, dying on, and at crises when I stand,
Say, on Ingpen Beacon eastward, or on Wylls-Neck
westwardly,
I seem where I was before my birth, and after death may be.

In the lowlands I have no comrade, not even the lone man's
friend—
Her who suffereth long and is kind; accepts what he is too
weak to mend:
Down there they are dubious and askance; there nobody
thinks as I,
But mind-chains do not clank where one's next neighbour is
the sky.

In the towns I am tracked by phantoms having weird detective
ways—
Shadows of beings who fellowed with myself of earlier days:
They hang about at places, and they say harsh heavy things—
Men with a wintry sneer, and women with tart disparagings.

Down there I seem to be false to myself, my simple self that
was,
And is not now, and I see him watching, wondering what
crass cause
Can have merged him into such a strange continuator as this,
Who yet has something in common with himself, my
chrysalis.

I cannot go to the great grey Plain; there's a figure against the
moon,
Nobody sees it but I, and it makes my breast beat out of tune;
I cannot go to the tall-spired town, being barred by the forms
now passed
For everybody but me, in whose long vision they stand there
fast.

There's a ghost at Yell'ham Bottom chiding loud at the fall of
the night,

There's a ghost in Froom-side Vale, thin-lipped and vague, in
a shroud of white,
There is one in the railway train whenever I do not want it
near,
I see its profile against the pane, saying what I would not hear.

As for one rare fair woman, I am now but a thought of hers,
I enter her mind and another thought succeeds me that she
prefers;
Yet my love for her in its fulness she herself even did not
know;
Well, time cures hearts of tenderness, and now I can let her
go.

So I am found on Ingpen Beacon, or on Wylls-Neck to the
west,
Or else on homely Bulbarrow, or little Pilsdon Crest,
Where men have never cared to haunt, nor women have
walked with me,
And ghosts then keep their distance; and I know some liberty.

In Death Divided

I

I shall rot here, with those whom in their day
        You never knew,
And alien ones who, ere they chilled to clay,
        Met not my view,
Will in your distant grave-place ever neighbour you.

II

No shade of pinnacle or tree or tower,
    While earth endures,
Will fall on my mound and within the hour
    Steal on to yours;
One robin never haunt our two green covertures.

III

Some organ may resound on Sunday noons
    By where you lie,
Some other thrill the panes with other tunes
    Where moulder I;
No selfsame chords compose our common lullaby.

IV

The simply-cut memorial at my head
    Perhaps may take
A rustic form, and that above your bed
    A stately make;
No linking symbol show thereon for our tale's sake.

V

And in the monotonous moils of strained, hard-run
    Humanity,
The eternal tie which binds us twain in one
    No eye will see
Stretching across the miles that sever you from me.
    189—

The Schreckhorn

With thoughts of Leslie Stephen, June 1897

Aloof, as if a thing of mood and whim;
Now that its spare and desolate figure gleams
Upon my nearing vision, less it seems
A looming Alp-height than a guise of him
Who scaled its horn with ventured life and limb,
Drawn on by vague imaginings, maybe,
Of semblance to his personality
In its quaint glooms, keen lights, and rugged trim.

At his last change, when Life's dull coils unwind,
Will he, in old love, hitherward escape,
And the eternal essence of his mind
Enter this silent adamantine shape,
And his low voicing haunt its slipping snows
When dawn that calls the climber dyes them rose?

Under the Waterfall

"Whenever I plunge my arm, like this,
In a basin of water, I never miss
The sweet sharp sense of a fugitive day
Fetched back from its thickening shroud of gray.
     hence the only prime
     And real love-rhyme
     That I know by heart,
     And that leaves no smart,
Is the purl of a little valley fall
About three spans wide and two spans tall

Over a table of solid rock,
And into a scoop of the self-same block;
The purl of a runlet that never ceases
In stir of kingdoms, in wars, in peaces;
With a hollow boiling voice it speaks
And has spoken since hills were turfless peaks."

"And why gives this the only prime
Idea to you of a real love-rhyme?
And why does plunging your arm in a bowl
Full of spring water, bring throbs to your soul?"

"Well, under the fall, in a crease of the stone,
Though where precisely none ever has known,
Jammed darkly, nothing to show how prized,
And by now with its smoothness opalized,
        Is a drinking-glass:
        For, down that pass
        My lover and I
        Walked under a sky
Of blue with a leaf-wove awning of green,
In the burn of August, to paint the scene,
And we placed our basket of fruit and wine
By the runlet's rim, where we sat to dine;
And when we had drunk from the glass together,
Arched by the oak-copse from the weather,
I held the vessel to rinse in the fall,
Where it slipped, and sank, and was past recall,
Though we stooped and plumbed the little abyss
With long bared arms. There the glass still is.
And, as said, if I thrust my arm below
Cold water in a basin or bowl, a throe
From the past awakens a sense of that time,

| 125 |

And the glass we used, and the cascade's rhyme.
The basin seems the pool, and its edge
The hard smooth face of the brook-side ledge,
And the leafy patterns of china-ware
The hanging plants that were bathing there.

"By night, by day, when it shines or lours,
There lies intact that chalice of ours,
And its presence adds to the rhyme of love
Persistently sung by the fall above.
No lip has touched it since his and mine
In turns therefrom sipped lovers' wine."

The Going

Why did you give no hint that night
That quickly after the morrow's dawn,
And calmly, as if indifferent quite,
You would close your term here, up and be gone
    Where I could not follow
    With wing of swallow
To gain one glimpse of you ever anon!

    Never to bid you good-bye,
    Or lip me the softest call,
Or utter a wish for a word, while I
Saw morning harden upon the wall,
    Unmoved, unknowing
    That your great going
Had place that moment, and altered all.

Why do you make me leave the house
And think for a breath it is you I see
At the end of the alley of bending boughs
Where so often at dusk you used to be;
    Till in darkening dankness
    The yawning blankness
Of the perspective sickens me!

    You were she who abode
    By those red-veined rocks far West,
You were the swan-necked one who rode
Along the beetling Beeny Crest,
    And, reining nigh me,
    Would muse and eye me,
While Life unrolled us its very best.

Why, then, latterly did we not speak,
Did we not think of those days long dead,
And ere your vanishing strive to seek
That time's renewal? We might have said,
    "In this bright spring weather
    We'll visit together
Those places that once we visited."

    Well, well! All's past amend,
    Unchangeable. It must go.
I seem but a dead man held on end
To sink down soon. . . . O you could not know
    That such swift fleeing
    No soul foreseeing—
Not even I—would undo me so!

Your Last Drive

Here by the moorway you returned,
And saw the borough lights ahead
That lit your face—all undiscerned
To be in a week the face of the dead,
And you told of the charm of that haloed view
That never again would beam on you.

And on your left you passed the spot
Where eight days later you were to lie,
And be spoken of as one who was not;
Beholding it with a heedless eye
As alien from you, though under its tree
You soon would halt everlastingly.

I drove not with you . . . Yet had I sat
At your side that eve I should not have seen
That the countenance I was glancing at
Had a last-time look in the flickering sheen,
Nor have read the writing upon your face,
"I go hence soon to my resting-place;

"You may miss me then. But I shall not know
How many times you visit me there,
Or what your thoughts are, or if you go
There never at all. And I shall not care.
Should you censure me I shall take no heed,
And even your praises no more shall need."

True: never you'll know. And you will not mind.
But shall I then slight you because of such?
Dear ghost, in the past did you ever find

The thought "What profit," move me much?
Yet abides the fact, indeed, the same,—
You are past love, praise, indifference, blame.

I Found Her Out There

I found her out there
On a slope few see,
That falls westwardly
To the salt-edged air,
Where the ocean breaks
On the purple strand,
And the hurricane shakes
The solid land.

I brought her here,
And have laid her to rest
In a noiseless nest
No sea beats near.
She will never be stirred
In her loamy cell
By the waves long heard
And loved so well.

So she does not sleep
By those haunted heights
The Atlantic smites
And the blind gales sweep,
Whence she often would gaze
At Dundagel's famed head,
While the dipping blaze
Dyed her face fire-red;

And would sigh at the tale
Of sunk Lyonnesse,
As a wind-tugged tress
Flapped her cheek like a flail;
Or listen at whiles
With a thought-bound brow
To the murmuring miles
She is far from now.

Yet her shade, maybe,
Will creep underground
Till it catch the sound
Of that western sea
As it swells and sobs
Where she once domiciled,
And joy in its throbs
With the heart of a child.

The Haunter

He does not think that I haunt here nightly:
    How shall I let him know
That whither his fancy sets him wandering
    I, too, alertly go?—
Hover and hover a few feet from him
    Just as I used to do,
But cannot answer the words he lifts me—
    Only listen thereto!

When I could answer he did not say them:
    When I could let him know

How I would like to join in his journeys
    Seldom he wished to go.
Now that he goes and wants me with him
    More than he used to do,
Never he sees my faithful phantom
    Though he speaks thereto.

Yes, I companion him to places
    Only dreamers know,
Where the shy hares print long paces,
    Where the night rooks go;
Into old aisles where the past is all to him,
    Close as his shade can do,
Always lacking the power to call to him,
    Near as I reach thereto!

What a good haunter I am, O tell him!
    Quickly make him know
If he but sigh since my loss befell him
    Straight to his side I go.
Tell him a faithful one is doing
    All that love can do
Still that his path may be worth pursuing,
    And to bring peace thereto.

The Voice

Woman much missed, how you call to me, call to me,
Saying that now you are not as you were
When you had changed from the one who was all to me,
But as at first, when our day was fair.

Can it be you that I hear? Let me view you, then,
Standing as when I drew near to the town
Where you would wait for me: yes, as I knew you then,
Even to the original air-blue gown!

Or is it only the breeze, in its listlessness
Travelling across the wet mead to me here,
You being ever dissolved to wan wistlessness,
Heard no more again far or near?

    Thus I; faltering forward,
    Leaves around me falling,
Wind oozing thin through the thorn from norward,
    And the woman calling.

After a Journey

Hereto I come to view a voiceless ghost;
    Whither, O whither will its whim now draw me?
Up the cliff, down, till I'm lonely, lost,
    And the unseen waters' ejaculations awe me.
Where you will next be there's no knowing,
    Facing round about me everywhere,
        With your nut-coloured hair,
And gray eyes, and rose-flush coming and going.

Yes: I have re-entered your olden haunts at last;
    Through the years, through the dead scenes I have tracked
you;
What have you now found to say of our past—
    Scanned across the dark space wherein I have lacked you?

Summer gave us sweets, but autumn wrought division?
    Things were not lastly as firstly well
        With us twain, you tell?
But all's closed now, despite Time's decision.

I see what you are doing: you are leading me on
    To the spots we knew when we haunted here together,
The waterfall, above which the mist-bow shone
    At the then fair hour in the then fair weather,
And the cave just under, with a voice still so hollow
    That it seems to call out to me from forty years ago,
        When you were all aglow,
And not the thin ghost that I now fraily follow!

Ignorant of what there is flitting here to see,
    The waked birds preen and the seals flop lazily;
Soon you will have, Dear, to vanish from me,
    For the stars close their shutters and the dawn whitens
hazily.
Trust me, I mind not, though Life lours,
    The bringing me here; nay, bring me here again!
        I am just the same as when
Our days were a joy, and our paths through flowers.

At Castle Boterel

As I drive to the junction of lane and highway,
    And the drizzle bedrenches the waggonnette,
I look behind at the fading byway,
    And see on its slope, now glistening wet,
        Distinctly yet

Myself and a girlish form benighted
   In dry March weather. We climb the road
Beside a chaise. We had just alighted
   To ease the sturdy pony's load
      When he sighed and slowed.

What we did as we climbed, and what we talked of
   Matters not much, nor to what it led,—
Something that life will not be balked of
   Without rude reason till hope is dead,
      And feeling fled.

It filled but a minute. But was there ever
   A time of such quality, since or before,
In that hill's story? To one mind never,
   Though it has been climbed, foot-swift, foot-sore,
      By thousands more.

Primaeval rocks form the road's steep border,
   And much have they faced there, first and last,
Of the transitory in Earth's long order;
   But what they record in colour and cast
      Is—that we two passed.

And to me, though Time's unflinching rigour,
   In mindless rote, has ruled from sight
The substance now, one phantom figure
   Remains on the slope, as when that night
      Saw us alight.

I look and see it there, shrinking, shrinking,
   I look back at it amid the rain

For the very last time; for my sand is sinking,
  And I shall traverse old love's domain
      Never again.

The Phantom Horsewoman

I

Queer are the ways of a man I know:
      He comes and stands
      In a careworn craze,
      And looks at the sands
      And the seaward haze
      With moveless hands
      And face and gaze,
      Then turns to go...
And what does he see when he gazes so?

II

They say he sees an instant thing
      More clear than to-day,
      A sweet soft scene
      That was once in play
      By that briny green;
      Yes, notes alway
      Warm, real, and keen,
      What his back years bring—
A phantom of his own figuring.

III

Of this vision of his they might say more:
                Not only there
                Does he see this sight,
                But everywhere
                In his brain—day, night,
                As if on the air
                It were drawn rose-bright—
                Yea, far from that shore
Does he carry this vision of heretofore:

IV

A ghost-girl-rider. And though, toil-tried,
                He withers daily,
                Time touches her not,
                But she still rides gaily
                In his rapt thought
                On that shagged and shaly
                Atlantic spot,
                And as when first eyed
Draws rein and sings to the swing of the tide.

Where the Picnic Was

        Where we made the fire
        In the summer time
        Of branch and briar
        On the hill to the sea,
        I slowly climb

Through winter mire,
And scan and trace
The forsaken place
Quite readily.

Now a cold wind blows,
And the grass is gray,
But the spot still shows
As a burnt circle—aye,
And stick-ends, charred,
Still strew the sward
Whereon I stand,
Last relic of the band
Who came that day!

Yes, I am here
Just as last year,
And the sea breathes brine
From its strange straight line
Up hither, the same
As when we four came.

—But two have wandered far
From this grassy rise
Into urban roar
Where no picnics are,
And one—has shut her eyes
For evermore.

The Newcomer's Wife

He paused on the sill of a door ajar
That screened a lively liquor-bar,
For the name had reached him through the door
Of her he had married the week before.

"We called her the Hack of the Parade;
But she was discreet in the games she played;
If slightly worn, she's pretty yet,
And gossips, after all, forget:

"And he knows nothing of her past;
I am glad the girl's in luck at last;
Such ones, though stale to native eyes,
Newcomers snatch at as a prize."

"Yes, being a stranger he sees her blent
Of all that's fresh and innocent,
Nor dreams how many a love-campaign
She had enjoyed before his reign!"

That night there was the splash of a fall
Over the slimy harbour-wall:
They searched, and at the deepest place
Found him with crabs upon his face.

Regret Not Me

Regret not me;
Beneath the sunny tree
I lie uncaring, slumbering peacefully.

Swift as the light
I flew my faery flight;
Ecstatically I moved, and feared no night.

I did not know
That heydays fade and go,
But deemed that what was would be always so.

I skipped at morn
Between the yellowing corn,
Thinking it good and glorious to be born.

I ran at eves
Among the piled-up sheaves,
Dreaming, "I grieve not, therefore nothing grieves."

Now soon will come
The apple, pear, and plum,
And hinds will sing, and autumn insects hum.

Again you will fare
To cider-makings rare,
And junketings; but I shall not be there.

Yet gaily sing
Under the pewter ring
Those songs we sang when we went gipsying.

And lightly dance
Some triple-timed romance
In coupled figures, and forget mischance;

And mourn not me
Beneath the yellowing tree;
For I shall mind not, slumbering peacefully.

Starlings on the Roof

"No smoke spreads out of this chimney-pot,
The people who lived here have left the spot,
And others are coming who knew them not.

"If you listen anon, with an ear intent,
The voices, you'll find, will be different
From the well-known ones of those who went."

"Why did they go? Their tones so bland
Were quite familiar to our band;
The comers we shall not understand."

"They look for a new life, rich and strange;
They do not know that, let them range
Wherever they may, they will get no change.

"They will drag their house-gear ever so far
In their search for a home no miseries mar;
They will find that as they were they are,

"That every hearth has a ghost, alack,
And can be but the scene of a bivouac
Till they move their last—no care to pack!"

The Two Soldiers

Just at the corner of the wall
    We met—yes, he and I—
Who had not faced in camp or hall
    Since we bade home good-bye,
And what once happened came back—all—
    Out of those years gone by;

And that strange woman whom we knew
    And loved—long dead and gone,
Whose poor half-perished residue,
    Tombless and trod, lay yon,
But at this moment to our view
    Rose like a phantom wan!

And in his fixed face I could see,
    Lit by a lurid shine,
The drama re-enact which she
    Had dyed incarnadine
For us, and more. And doubtless he
    Beheld it too in mine.

A start, as at one slightly known;
    And with an indifferent air
We passed, without a sign being shown
    That, as it real were,
A memory-acted scene had thrown
    Its tragic shadow there.

The Roman Gravemounds

By Rome's dim relics there walks a man,
Eyes bent; and he carries a basket and spade;
I guess what impels him to scrape and scan;
Yea, his dreams of that Empire long decayed.

"Vast was Rome," he must muse, "in the world's regard,
Vast it looms there still, vast it ever will be;"
And he stoops as to dig and unmine some shard
Left by those who are held in such memory.

But no; in his basket, see, he has brought
A little white furred thing, stiff of limb,
Whose life never won from the world a thought;
It is this, and not Rome, that is moving him.

And to make it a grave he has come to the spot,
And he delves in the ancient dead's long home;
Their fames, their achievements, the man knows not;
The furred thing is all to him—nothing Rome!

"Here you say that Cæsar's warriors lie?—
But my little white cat was my only friend!
Could she but live, might the record die
Of Cæsar, his legions, his aims, his end!"

Well, Rome's long rule here is oft and again
A theme for the sages of history,
And the small furred life was worth no one's pen;
Yet its mourner's mood has a charm for me.

The Satin Shoes

"If ever I walk to church to wed,
    As other maidens use,
And face the gathered eyes," she said,
    "I'll go in satin shoes!"

She was as fair as early day
    Shining on meads unmown,
And her sweet syllables seemed to play
    Like flute-notes softly blown.

The time arrived when it was meet
    That she should be a bride;
The satin shoes were on her feet,
    Her father was at her side.

They stood within the dairy door,
    And gazed across the green;
The church loomed on the distant moor,
    But rain was thick between.

"The grass-path hardly can be stepped,
    The lane is like a pool!"—
Her dream is shown to be inept,
    Her wish they overrule.

"To go forth shod in satin soft
    A coach would be required!"
For thickest boots the shoes were doffed—
    Those shoes her soul desired. . . .

All day the bride, as overborne,
    Was seen to brood apart,
And that the shoes had not been worn
    Sat heavy on her heart.

From her wrecked dream, as months flew on,
    Her thought seemed not to range.
"What ails the wife," they said anon,
    "That she should be so strange?". . .

Ah—what coach comes with furtive glide—
    A coach of closed-up kind?
It comes to fetch the last year's bride,
    Who wanders in her mind.

She strove with them, and fearfully ran
    Stairward with one low scream:
"Nay—coax her," said the madhouse man,
    "With some old household theme."

"If you will go, dear, you must fain
    Put on these shoes—the pair
Meant for your marriage, which the rain
    Forbade you then to wear."

She clapped her hands, flushed joyous hues;
    "O yes—I'll up and ride
If I am to wear my satin shoes
    And be a proper bride!"

Out then her little foot held she,
    As to depart with speed;

The madhouse man smiled pleasantly
 	To see the wile succeed.

She turned to him when all was done,
 	And gave him her thin hand,
Exclaiming like an enraptured one,
 	"This time it will be grand!"

She mounted with a face elate,
 	Shut was the carriage door;
They drove her to the madhouse gate,
 	And she was seen no more. . . .

Yet she was fair as early day
 	Shining on meads unmown,
And her sweet syllables seemed to play
 	Like flute-notes softly blown.

Afterwards

When the Present has latched its postern behind my tremulous stay,
 	And the May month flaps its glad green leaves like wings,
Delicate-filmed as new-spun silk, will the neighbours say,
 	"He was a man who used to notice such things"?

If it be in the dusk when, like an eyelid's soundless blink,
 	The dewfall-hawk comes crossing the shades to alight
Upon the wind-warped upland thorn, a gazer may think,
 	"To him this must have been a familiar sight."

If I pass during some nocturnal blackness, mothy and warm,
    When the hedgehog travels furtively over the lawn.
One may say, "He strove that such innocent creatures should
come to no harm,
    But he could do little for them; and now he is gone."

If, when hearing that I have been stilled at last, they stand at
the door,
    Watching the full-starred heavens that winter sees,
Will this thought rise on those who will meet my face no
more,
    "He was one who had an eye for such mysteries"?

And will any say when my bell of quittance is heard in the
gloom,
    And a crossing breeze cuts a pause in its outrollings,
Till they rise again, as they were a new bell's boom,
    "He hears it not now, but used to notice such things"?

In the Moonlight

    "O lonely workman, standing there
    In a dream, why do you stare and stare
    At her grave, as no other grave there were?

    "If your great gaunt eyes so importune
    Her soul by the shine of this corpse-cold moon
    Maybe you'll raise her phantom soon!"

    "Why, fool, it is what I would rather see
    Than all the living folk there be;
    But alas, there is no such joy for me!"

"Ah—she was one you loved, no doubt,
Through good and evil, through rain and drought,
And when she passed, all your sun went out?"

"Nay: she was the woman I did not love,
Whom all the others were ranked above,
Whom during her life I thought nothing of."

In a Museum

I

Here's the mould of a musical bird long passed from light,
Which over the earth before man came was winging;
There's a contralto voice I heard last night,
That lodges in me still with its sweet singing.

II

Such a dream is Time that the coo of this ancient bird
Has perished not, but is blent, or will be blending
Mid visionless wilds of space with the voice that I heard,
In the full-fugued song of the universe unending.

Heredity

I am the family face;
Flesh perishes, I live on,
Projecting trait and trace
Through time to times anon,

And leaping from place to place
Over oblivion.

The years-heired feature that can
In curve and voice and eye
Despise the human span
Of durance—that is I;
The eternal thing in man,
That heeds no call to die.

Near Lanivet, 1872

There was a stunted handpost just on the crest,
        Only a few feet high:
She was tired, and we stopped in the twilight-time for her rest,
        At the crossways close thereby.

She leant back, being so weary, against its stem,
        And laid her arms on its own,
Each open palm stretched out to each end of them,
        Her sad face sideways thrown.

Her white-clothed form at this dim-lit cease of day
        Made her look as one crucified
In my gaze at her from the midst of the dusty way,
        And hurriedly "Don't," I cried.

I do not think she heard. Loosing thence she said,
        As she stepped forth ready to go,
"I am rested now.—Something strange came into my head;
        I wish I had not leant so!"

And wordless we moved onward down from the hill
      In the west cloud's murked obscure,
And looking back we could see the handpost still
      In the solitude of the moor.

"It struck her too," I thought, for as if afraid
      She heavily breathed as we trailed;
Till she said, "I did not think how 'twould look in the shade,
      When I leant there like one nailed."

I, lightly: "There's nothing in it. For *you,* anyhow!"
      —"O I know there is not," said she . . .
"Yet I wonder . . . If no one is bodily crucified now,
      In spirit one may be!"

And we dragged on and on, while we seemed to see
      In the running of Time's far glass
Her crucified, as she had wondered if she might be
      Some day.— Alas, alas!

Timing Her

Written to an old folk-tune

      Lalage's coming:
      Where is she now, O?
      Turning to bow, O,
      And smile, is she,
      Just at parting,
      Parting, parting,
      As she is starting
      To come to me?

Where is she now, O,
Now, and now, O,
Shadowing a bough, O,
Of hedge or tree
As she is rushing,
Rushing, rushing,
Gossamers brushing
To come to me?

Lalage's coming;
Where is she now, O;
Climbing the brow, O,
Of hills I see?
Yes, she is nearing,
Nearing, nearing,
Weather unfearing
To come to me.

Near is she now, O,
Now, and now, O;
Milk the rich cow, O,
Forward the tea;
Shake the down bed for her,
Linen sheets spread for her,
Drape round the head for her
Coming to me.

Lalage's coming,
She's nearer now, O,
End anyhow, O,
To-day's husbandry!
Would a gilt chair were mine,

Slippers of vair were mine,
Brushes for hair were mine
Of ivory!

What will she think, O,
She who's so comely,
Viewing how homely
A sort are we!
Nothing resplendent,
No prompt attendant,
Not one dependent
Pertaining to me!

Lalage's coming;
Where is she now, O?
Fain I'd avow, O,
Full honestly
Nought here's enough for her,
All is too rough for her,
Even my love for her
Poor in degree.

She's nearer now, O,
Still nearer now, O,
She 'tis, I vow, O,
Passing the lea.
Rush down to meet her there,
Call out and greet her there,
Never a sweeter there
Crossed to me!

Lalage's come; aye,
Come is she now, O!...
Does Heaven allow, O,
A meeting to be?
Yes, she is here now,
Here now, here now,
Nothing to fear now,
Here's Lalage!

The Oxen

Christmas Eve, and twelve of the clock.
   "Now they are all on their knees,"
An elder said as we sat in a flock
   By the embers in hearthside ease.

We pictured the meek mild creatures where
   They dwelt in their strawy pen,
Nor did it occur to one of us there
   To doubt they were kneeling then.

So fair a fancy few would weave
   In those years! Yet, I feel,
If someone said on Christmas Eve,
   "Come; see the oxen kneel

"In the lonely barton by yonder coomb
   Our childhood used to know,"
I should go with him in the gloom,
   Hoping it might be so.

Transformations

Portion of this yew
Is a man my grandsire knew,
Bosomed here at its foot:
This branch may be his wife,
A ruddy human life
Now turned to a green shoot.

These grasses must be made
Of her who often prayed,
Last century, for repose;
And the fair girl long ago
Whom I often tried to know
May be entering this rose.

So, they are not underground,
But as nerves and veins abound
In the growths of upper air,
And they feel the sun and rain,
And the energy again
That made them what they were!

The Last Signal

A Memory of William Barnes

Silently I footed by an uphill road
  That led from my abode to a spot yew-boughed;
Yellowly the sun sloped low down to westward,
    And dark was the east with cloud.

Then, amid the shadow of that livid sad east,
   Where the light was least, and a gate stood wide,
Something flashed the fire of the sun that was facing it,
      Like a brief blaze on that side.

Looking hard and harder I knew what it meant—
   The sudden shine sent from the livid east scene;
It meant the west mirrored by the coffin of my friend there,
      Turning to the road from his green,

To take his last journey forth—he who in his prime
   Trudged so many a time from that gate athwart the land!
Thus a farewell to me he signalled on his grave-way,
      As with a wave of his hand.

Old Furniture

I know not how it may be with others
      Who sit amid relics of householdry
That date from the days of their mothers' mothers,
      But well I know how it is with me
         Continually.

I see the hands of the generations
      That owned each shiny familiar thing
In play on its knobs and indentations,
      And with its ancient fashioning
         Still dallying:

Hands behind hands, growing paler and paler,
      As in a mirror a candle-flame

Shows images of itself, each frailer
    As it recedes, though the eye may frame
      Its shape the same.

On the clock's dull dial a foggy finger,
    Moving to set the minutes right
With tentative touches that lift and linger
    In the wont of a moth on a summer night,
      Creeps to my sight.

On this old viol, too, fingers are dancing—
    As whilom—just over the strings by the nut,
The tip of a bow receding, advancing
    In airy quivers, as if it would cut
      The plaintive gut.

And I see a face by that box for tinder,
    Glowing forth in fits from the dark,
And fading again, as the linten cinder
    Kindles to red at the flinty spark,
      Or goes out stark.

Well, well. It is best to be up and doing,
    The world has no use for one to-day
Who eyes things thus—no aim pursuing!
    He should not continue in this stay,
      But sink away.

During Wind and Rain

They sing their dearest songs—

He, she, all of them—yea,
Treble and tenor and bass,
    And one to play;
With the candles mooning each face. . . .
    Ah, no; the years O!
How the sick leaves reel down in throngs!

They clear the creeping moss—
Elders and juniors—aye,
Making the pathways neat
    And the garden gay;
And they build a shady seat. . . .
    Ah, no; the years, the years;
See, the white storm-birds wing across!

They are blithely breakfasting all—
Men and maidens—yea,
Under the summer tree,
    With a glimpse of the bay,
While pet fowl come to the knee. . . .
    Ah, no; the years O!
And the rotten rose is ript from the wall.

They change to a high new house,
He, she, all of them—aye,
Clocks and carpets and chairs
    On the lawn all day,
And brightest things that are theirs. . . .
    Ah, no; the years, the years;
Down their carved names the rain-drop ploughs.

For Life I Had Never Cared Greatly

For Life I had never cared greatly,
    As worth a man's while;
      Peradventures unsought,
    Peradventures that finished in nought,
Had kept me from youth and through manhood till lately
        Unwon by its style.

In earliest years—why I know not—
    I viewed it askance;
      Conditions of doubt,
    Conditions that leaked slowly out,
May haply have bent me to stand and to show not
        Much zest for its dance.

With symphonies soft and sweet colour
    It courted me then,
      Till evasions seemed wrong,
    Till evasions gave in to its song,
And I warmed, until living aloofly loomed duller
        Than life among men.

Anew I found nought to set eyes on,
    When, lifting its hand,
      It uncloaked a star,
    Uncloaked it from fog-damps afar,
And showed its beams burning from pole to horizon
        As bright as a brand.

And so, the rough highway forgetting,
    I pace hill and dale

Regarding the sky,
Regarding the vision on high,
And thus re-illumed have no humour for letting
My pilgrimage fail.

The Pity of It

I walked in loamy Wessex lanes, afar
From rail-track and from highway, and I heard
In field and farmstead many an ancient word
Of local lineage like "Thu bist," "Er war,"

"Ich woll," "Er sholl," and by-talk similar,
Nigh as they speak who in this month's moon gird
At England's very loins, thereunto spurred
By gangs whose glory threats and slaughters are.

Then seemed a Heart crying: "Whosoever they be
At root and bottom of this, who flung this flame
Between kin folk kin tongued even as are we,

"Sinister, ugly, lurid, be their fame;
May their familiars grow to shun their name,
And their brood perish everlastingly."

In Time of "The Breaking of Nations"

I

Only a man harrowing clods
In a slow silent walk

| 158 |

With an old horse that stumbles and nods
    Half asleep as they stalk.

II

Only thin smoke without flame
    From the heaps of couch-grass;
Yet this will go onward the same
    Though Dynasties pass.

III

Yonder a maid and her wight
    Come whispering by:
War's annals will cloud into night
    Ere their story die.

I Looked Up from My Writing

I looked up from my writing,
    And gave a start to see,
As if rapt in my inditing,
    The moon's full gaze on me.

Her meditative misty head
    Was spectral in its air,
And I involuntarily said,
    "What are you doing there?"

"Oh, I've been scanning pond and hole
    And waterway hereabout

| 159 |

For the body of one with a sunken soul
    Who has put his life-light out.

"Did you hear his frenzied tattle?
    It was sorrow for his son
Who is slain in brutish battle,
    Though he has injured none.

"And now I am curious to look
    Into the blinkered mind
Of one who wants to write a book
    In a world of such a kind."

Her temper overwrought me,
    And I edged to shun her view,
For I felt assured she thought me
    One who should drown him too.

Going and Staying

I

The moving sun-shapes on the spray,
The sparkles where the brook was flowing,
Pink faces, plightings, moonlit May,
These were the things we wished would stay;
    But they were going.

II

Seasons of blankness as of snow,
The silent bleed of a world decaying,

The moan of multitudes in woe,
These were the things we wished would go;
    But they were staying.

III

Then we looked closelier at Time,
And saw his ghostly arms revolving
To sweep off woeful things with prime,
Things sinister with things sublime
    Alike dissolving.

"And There Was a Great Calm"

On the Signing of the Armistice, 11 Nov. 1918

I

There had been years of Passion—scorching, cold,
And much Despair, and Anger heaving high,
Care whitely watching, Sorrows manifold,
Among the young, among the weak and old,
And the pensive Spirit of Pity whispered, "Why?"

II

Men had not paused to answer. Foes distraught
Pierced the thinned peoples in a brute-like blindness,
Philosophies that sages long had taught,
And Selflessness, were as an unknown thought,
And "Hell!" and "Shell!" were yapped at Lovingkindness.

III

The feeble folk at home had grown full-used
To "dug-outs," "snipers," "Huns," from the war-adept
In the mornings heard, and at evetides perused;
To day-dreamt men in millions, when they mused—
To nightmare-men in millions when they slept.

IV

Waking to wish existence timeless, null,
Sirius they watched above where armies fell;
He seemed to check his flapping when, in the lull
Of night a boom came thencewise, like the dull
Plunge of a stone dropped into some deep well.

V

So, when old hopes that earth was bettering slowly
Were dead and damned, there sounded "War is done!"
One morrow. Said the bereft, and meek, and lowly,
"Will men some day be given to grace? yea, wholly,
And in good sooth, as our dreams used to run?"

VI

Breathless they paused. Out there men raised their glance
To where had stood those poplars lank and lopped,
As they had raised it through the four years' dance
Of Death in the now familiar flats of France;
And murmured, "Strange, this! How? All firing stopped?"

VII

Aye; all was hushed. The about-to-fire fired not,
The aimed-at moved away in trance-lipped song.
One checkless regiment slung a clinching shot
And turned. The Spirit of Irony smirked out, "What?
Spoil peradventures woven of Rage and Wrong?"

VIII

Thenceforth no flying fires inflamed the gray,
No hurtlings shook the dewdrop from the thorn,
No moan perplexed the mute bird on the spray;
Worn horses mused: "We are not whipped to-day";
No weft-winged engines blurred the moon's thin horn.

IX

Calm fell. From Heaven distilled a clemency;
There was peace on earth, and silence in the sky;
Some could, some could not, shake off misery:
The Sinister Spirit sneered: "It had to be!"
And again the Spirit of Pity whispered, "Why?"

Haunting Fingers

A Phantasy in a Museum of Musical Instruments

"Are you awake,
   Comrades, this silent night?
Well, 'twere if all of our glossy gluey make
Lay in the damp without, and fell to fragments quite!"

"O viol, my friend,
  I watch, though Phosphor nears,
And I fain would drowse away to its utter end
This dumb dark stowage after our loud melodious years!"

And they felt past handlers clutch them,
  Though none was in the room,
Old players' dead fingers touch them,
    Shrunk in the tomb.

  "'Cello, good mate,
  You speak my mind as yours:
Doomed to this voiceless, crippled, corpselike state,
Who, dear to famed Amphion, trapped here, long endures?"

  "Once I could thrill
  The populace through and through,
Wake them to passioned pulsings past their will.". . .
(A contra-basso spake so, and the rest sighed anew.)

And they felt old muscles travel
  Over their tense contours,
And with long skill unravel
  Cunningest scores.

  "The tender pat
  Of her aery finger-tips
Upon me daily—I rejoiced thereat!"
(Thuswise a harpsichord, as 'twere from dampered lips.)

  "My keys' white shine,
  Now sallow, met a hand

Even whiter. . . . Tones of hers fell forth with mine
In sowings of sound so sweet no lover could withstand!"

And its clavier was filmed with fingers
    Like tapering flames—wan, cold—
Or the nebulous light that lingers
        In charnel mould.

        "Gayer than most
    Was I," reverbed a drum;
    "The regiments, marchings, throngs, hurrahs! What a host
I stirred—even when crape mufflings gagged me well-nigh
dumb!"

        Trilled an aged viol:
    "Much tune have I set free
    To spur the dance, since my first timid trial
Where I had birth—far hence, in sun-swept Italy!"

And he feels apt touches on him
    From those that pressed him then;
Who seem with their glance to con him,
    Saying, "Not again!"

        "A holy calm,"
    Mourned a shawm's voice subdued,
    "Steeped my Cecilian rhythms when hymns and psalm
Poured from devout souls met in Sabbath sanctitude."

        "I faced the sock
    Nightly," twanged a sick lyre,
    "Over ranked lights! O charm of life in mock,
O scenes that fed love, hope, wit, rapture, mirth, desire!"

Thus they, till each past player
   Stroked thinner and more thin,
And the morning sky grew grayer
   And day crawled in.

The Selfsame Song

A bird sings the selfsame song,
With never a fault in its flow,
That we listened to here those long
     Long years ago.

A pleasing marvel is how
A strain of such rapturous rote
Should have gone on thus till now
     Unchanged in a note!

—But it's not the selfsame bird.—
No: perished to dust is he. . . .
As also are those who heard
     That song with me.

At Lulworth Cove a Century Back

Had I but lived a hundred years ago
I might have gone, as I have gone this year,
By Warmwell Cross on to a Cove I know,
And Time have placed his finger on me there:

"You see that man?"—I might have looked, and said,
"O yes: I see him. One that boat has brought
Which dropped down Channel round Saint Alban's Head.
So commonplace a youth calls not my thought."

"You see that man?"—"Why yes: I told you; yes:
Of an idling town-sort; thin; hair brown in hue;
And as the evening light scants less and less
He looks up at a star, as many do."

"You see that man?"—"Nay, leave me!" then I plead,
"I have fifteen miles to vamp across the lea,
And it grows dark, and I am weary-kneed:
I have said the third time; yes, that man I see!"

"Good. That man goes to Rome—to death, despair;
And no one notes him now but you and I:
A hundred years, and the world will follow him there,
And bend with reverence where his ashes lie."

NOTE—*In September 1820 Keats, on his way to Rome, landed one day on the Dorset coast, and composed the sonnet, "Bright Star! would I were as steadfast as thou art!" The spot of his landing is judged to have been Lulworth Cove.*

Evelyn G. of Christminster

I can see the towers
In mind quite clear
Not many hours'
Faring from here;
But how up and go,

And briskly bear
Thither, and know
That you are not there?

Though the birds sing small,
And apple and pear
On your trees by the wall
Are ripe and rare,
Though none excel them,
I have no care
To taste them or smell them
And you were not there.

Though the College stones
Are stroked with the sun,
And the gownsmen and Dons
Who held you as one
Of brightest brow
Still think as they did,
Why haunt with them now
Your candle is hid?

Towards the river
A pealing swells:
They cost me a quiver—
Those prayerful bells!
How to go to God,
Who can reprove
With so heavy a rod
As your swift remove!

The chorded keys
Wait all in a row,
And the bellows wheeze
As long ago.
And the psalter lingers,
And organist's chair;
But where are your fingers
That once wagged there?

Shall I then seek
That desert place
This or next week,
And those tracks trace
That fill me with cark
And cloy; nowhere
Being movement or mark
Of you now there!

By Henstridge Cross at the Year's End

From this centuries-old cross-road the highway leads east to London, north to Bristol and Bath, west to Exeter and the Land's End, and south to the Channel coast.

Why go the east road now?. . .
That way a youth went on a morrow
After mirth, and he brought back sorrow
Painted upon his brow:
Why go the east road now?

Why go the north road now?
Torn, leaf-strewn, as if scoured by foemen,
Once edging fiefs of my forefolk yeomen,
    Fallows fat to the plough:
    Why go the north road now?

Why go the west road now?
Thence to us came she, bosom-burning,
Welcome with joyousness returning. . . .
    She sleeps under the bough:
    Why go the west road now?

Why go the south road now?
That way marched they some are forgetting,
Stark to the moon left, past regretting
    Loves who have failed their vow. . . .
    Why go the south road now?

Why go any road now?
White stands the handpost for brisk onbearers,
"Halt!" is the word for wan-cheeked farers
    Musing on Whither, and How. . . .
    Why go any road now?

"Yea: we want new feet now"
Answer the stones. "Want chit-chat, laughter:
Plenty of such to go hereafter
    By our tracks, we trow!
    We are for new feet now."

Vagg Hollow

"What do you see in Vagg Hollow,
Little boy, when you go
In the morning at five on your lonely drive?"
"—I see men's souls, who follow
Till we've passed where the road lies low,
When they vanish at our creaking!

"They are like white faces speaking
Beside and behind the waggon—
One just as father's was when here.
The waggoner drinks from his flagon,
(Or he'd flinch when the Hollow is near)
But he does not give me any.

"Sometimes the faces are many;
But I walk along by the horses,
He asleep on the straw as we jog;
And I hear the loud water-courses,
And the drops from the trees in the fog,
And watch till the day is breaking,

"And the wind out by Tintinhull waking;
I hear in it father's call
As he called when I saw him dying,
And he sat by the fire last Fall,
And mother stood by sighing;
But I'm not afraid at all!"

First or Last

Song

If grief come early
Joy comes late,
If joy come early
Grief will wait;
   Aye, my dear and tender!

Wise ones joy them early
While the cheeks are red,
Banish grief till surly
Time has dulled their dread.

   And joy being ours
   Ere youth has flown,
   The later hours
   May find us gone;
      Aye, my dear and tender!

In a London Flat

I

"You look like a widower," she said
Through the folding-doors with a laugh from the bed,
As he sat by the fire in the outer room,
Reading late on a night of gloom,
And a cab-hack's wheeze, and the clap of its feet
In its breathless pace on the smooth wet street,

Were all that came to them now and then. . . .
"You really do!" she quizzed again.

II

And the Spirits behind the curtains heard,
And also laughed, amused at her word,
And at her light-hearted view of him.
"Let's get him made so—just for a whim!"
Said the Phantom Ironic. "'Twould serve her right
If we coaxed the Will to do it some night."
"O pray not!" pleaded the younger one,
The Sprite of the Pities. "She said it in fun!"

III

But so it befell, whatever the cause,
That what she had called him he next year was;
And on such a night, when she lay elsewhere,
He, watched by those Phantoms, again sat there,
And gazed, as if gazing on far faint shores,
At the empty bed through the folding-doors
As he remembered her words; and wept
That she had forgotten them where she slept.

An Ancient to Ancients

Where once we danced, where once we sang,
        Gentlemen,
The floors are sunken, cobwebs hang,
And cracks creep; worms have fed upon

The doors. Yea, sprightlier times were then
Than now, with harps and tabrets gone,
          Gentlemen!

Where once we rowed, where once we sailed,
          Gentlemen,
And damsels took the tiller, veiled
Against too strong a stare (God wot
Their fancy, then or anywhen!)
Upon that shore we are clean forgot,
          Gentlemen!

We have lost somewhat, afar and near,
          Gentlemen,
The thinning of our ranks each year
Affords a hint we are nigh undone,
That we shall not be ever again
The marked of many, loved of one,
          Gentlemen.

In dance the polka hit our wish,
          Gentlemen,
The paced quadrille, the spry schottische,
"Sir Roger."—And in opera spheres
The "Girl" (the famed "Bohemian"),
And "Trovatore," held the ears,
          Gentlemen.

This season's paintings do not please,
          Gentlemen,
Like Etty, Mulready, Maclise;
Throbbing romance has waned and wanned;

No wizard wields the witching pen
Of Bulwer, Scott, Dumas, and Sand,
   Gentlemen.

The bower we shrined to Tennyson,
   Gentlemen,
Is roof-wrecked; damps there drip upon
Sagged seats, the creeper-nails are rust,
The spider is sole denizen;
Even she who voiced those rhymes is dust,
   Gentlemen!

We who met sunrise sanguine-souled,
   Gentlemen,
Are wearing weary. We are old;
These younger press; we feel our rout
Is imminent to Aïdes' den,—
That evening shades are stretching out,
   Gentlemen!

And yet, though ours be failing frames,
   Gentlemen,
So were some others' history names,
Who trode their track light-limbed and fast
As these youth, and not alien
From enterprise, to their long last,
   Gentlemen.

Sophocles, Plato, Socrates,
   Gentlemen,
Pythagoras, Thucydides,
Herodotus, and Homer,—yea,

Clement, Augustin, Origen,
Burnt brightlier towards their setting-day,
     Gentlemen.

And ye, red-lipped and smooth-browed; list,
     Gentlemen;
Much is there waits you we have missed;
Much lore we leave you worth the knowing,
Much, much has lain outside our ken:
Nay, rush not: time serves: we are going,
     Gentlemen.

When Dead

To ———

It will be much better when
    I am under the bough;
I shall be more myself, Dear, then,
    Than I am now.

No sign of querulousness
    To wear you out
Shall I show there: strivings and stress
    Be quite without.

This fleeting life-brief blight
    Will have gone past
When I resume my old and right
    Place in the Vast.

And when you come to me
To show you true,
Doubt not I shall infallibly
Be waiting you.

No Buyers

A Street Scene

A load of brushes and baskets and cradles and chairs
　　Labours along the street in the rain:
With it a man, a woman, a pony with whiteybrown hairs.—
　　The man foots in front of the horse with a shambling
sway
　　　　At a slower tread than a funeral train,
　　While to a dirge-like tune he chants his wares,
Swinging a Turk's-head brush (in a drum-major's way
　　　　When the bandsmen march and play).

A yard from the back of the man is the whiteybrown pony's
nose:
He mirrors his master in every item of pace and pose:
　　　　He stops when the man stops, without being told,
　　And seems to be eased by a pause; too plainly he's old,
　　　　Indeed, not strength enough shows

　　　　To steer the disjointed waggon straight,
　　Which wriggles left and right in a rambling line,
　　Deflected thus by its own warp and weight,
　　And pushing the pony with it in each incline.

The woman walks on the pavement verge,
　　　　Parallel to the man:
She wears an apron white and wide in span,
And carries a like Turk's-head, but more in nursing-wise:
　　　　Now and then she joins in his dirge,
　　　　But as if her thoughts were on distant things.
　　　　The rain claims her apron till it clings.—
So, step by step, they move with their merchandize,
　　　　And nobody buys.

Nobody Comes

Tree-leaves labour up and down,
　　　　And through them the fainting light
　　　　Succumbs to the crawl of night.
Outside in the road the telegraph wire
　　　　To the town from the darkening land
Intones to travellers like a spectral lyre
　　　　Swept by a spectral hand.

A car comes up, with lamps full-glare,
　　　　That flash upon a tree:
　　　　It has nothing to do with me,
And whangs along in a world of its own,
　　　　Leaving a blacker air;
And mute by the gate I stand again alone,
　　　　And nobody pulls up there.

Horses Aboard

Horses in horsecloths stand in a row
On board the huge ship, that at last lets go:
Whither are they sailing? They do not know,
Nor what for, nor how.—
　　　　　　They are horses of war,
And are going to where there is fighting afar;
But they gaze through their eye-holes unwitting they are,
And that in some wilderness, gaunt and ghast,
Their bones will bleach ere a year has passed,
And the item be as "war-waste" classed.—
And when the band booms, and the folk say "Good-bye!"
And the shore slides astern, they appear wrenched awry
From the scheme Nature planned for them,—wondering why.

The Missed Train

　　How I was caught
Hieing home, after days of allure,
And forced to an inn—small, obscure—
　　At the junction, gloom-fraught.

　　How civil my face
To get them to chamber me there—
A roof I had scorned, scarce aware
　　That it stood at the place.

　　And how all the night
I had dreams of the unwitting cause
Of my lodgment. How lonely I was;
　　How consoled by her sprite!

| 179 |

Thus onetime to me...
Dim wastes of dead years bar away
Then from now. But such happenings to-day
    Fall to lovers, may be!

Years, years as shoaled seas,
Truly, stretch now between! Less and less
Shrink the visions then vast in me.—Yes,
    Then in me: Now in these.

Epitaph on a Pessimist

From the French and Greek

I'm Smith of Stoke, aged sixty-odd,
    I've lived without a dame
From youth-time on; and would to God
    My dad had done the same.

The Protean Maiden

Song

This single girl is two girls:
    How strange such things should be!
One noon eclipsed by few girls,
    The next no beauty she.

And daily cries the lover,
    In voice and feature vext:
"My last impression of her
    Is never to be the next!

"She's plain: I will forget her!
   She's turned to fair. Ah no,
Forget?—not I! I'll pet her
   With kisses swift and slow."

The Rover Come Home

He's journeyed through America
   From Canso Cape to Horn,
And from East Indian Comorin
   To Behring's Strait forlorn;
He's felled trees in the backwoods,
   In swamps has gasped for breath;
In Tropic heats, in Polar ice,
   Has often prayed for death.

He has fought and bled in civil wars
   Of no concern to him,
Has shot his fellows—beasts and men—
   At risk of life and limb.
He has suffered fluxes, fevers,
   Agues, and ills allied,
And now he's home. You look at him
   As he talks by your fireside.

And what is written in his glance
   Stressed by such foreign wear,
After such alien circumstance
   What does his face declare?
His mother's; she who saw him not
   After his starting year,

Who never left her native spot,
And lies in the churchyard near.

Lying Awake

You, Morningtide Star, now are steady-eyed, over the east,
I know it as if I saw you;
You, Beeches, engrave on the sky your thin twigs, even the
least;
Had I paper and pencil I'd draw you.

You, Meadow, are white with your counterpane cover of
dew,
I see it as if I were there;
You, Churchyard, are lightening faint from the shade of the
yew,
The names creeping out everywhere.

We Say We Shall Not Meet

We say we shall not meet
Again beneath this sky,
And turn with leaden feet,
Murmuring "Good-bye!"

But laugh at how we rued
Our former time's adieu
When those who went for good
Are met anew.

We talk in lightest vein
On trifles talked before,
And part to meet again,
    But meet no more.

Christmas: 1924

"Peace upon earth!" was said. We sing it,
And pay a million priests to bring it.
After two thousand years of mass
We've got as far as poison-gas.

How She Went to Ireland

Dora's gone to Ireland
   Through the sleet and snow;
Promptly she has gone there
   In a ship, although
Why she's gone to Ireland
   Dora does not know.

That was where, yea, Ireland,
   Dora wished to be:
When she felt, in lone times,
   Shoots of misery,
Often there, in Ireland,
   Dora wished to be.

Hence she's gone to Ireland,
   Since she meant to go,

Through the drift and darkness
Onward labouring, though
That she's gone to Ireland
Dora does not know.

He Resolves to Say No More

O my soul, keep the rest unknown!
It is too like a sound of moan
When the charnel-eyed
Pale Horse has nighed:
Yea, none shall gather what I hide!

Why load men's minds with more to bear
That bear already ails to spare?
From now alway
Till my last day
What I discern I will not say.

Let Time roll backward if it will;
(Magians who drive the midnight quill
With brain aglow
Can see it so,)
What I have learnt no man shall know.

And if my vision range beyond
The blinkered sight of souls in bond,
—By truth made free—
I'll let all be,
And show to no man what I see.